The World of the
ONEDIN LINE

The World of the
ONEDIN LINE

Alison McLeay

David & Charles
Newton Abbot · London · North Pomfret (Vt) · Vancouver

ISBN 0 7153 7398 6

© Alison McLeay 1977

First published June 1977
Reprinted October 1977

Set in 11 on 12-point Plantin
and printed and bound in Great Britain
by Morrison & Gibb Limited, London and Edinburgh
for David & Charles (Publishers) Limited
Brunel House Newton Abbot Devon

Published in the United States of America
by David & Charles Inc
North Pomfret Vermont 05053 USA

Published in Canada
by Douglas David & Charles Limited
1875 Welch Street North Vancouver BC

Contents

Introduction

What is it that makes a television series as welcome in Jamaican homes as it is round a British or Dutch fireside or in the air-conditioned apartments of Saudi Arabia?

It seems almost incredible that any television programme should have such universal appeal, especially when its story is set in the commercial world of late nineteenth-century Liverpool. Yet this is the achievement of BBC Television's long-running series *The Onedin Line*, as popular in countries all over the globe as it is in the heart of Merseyside itself.

The secret, surely, is the spell which the sea has always cast over the shore-bound: there is magic not only in the graceful form of a tall ship under sail, but even in the prosaic shape of a rust-streaked coaster, a tiny self-sufficient world heading out of port towards a mysterious horizon.

This book is written for anyone who has felt the lure of the sea, even if his or her closest contact with it has been through the adventures of the Onedins and their ships. I hope it gives some idea of the realities of seafaring in the days when the beauty of the sailing-ships contrasted sharply with the unbelievably hard lives led by their crews; I hope it also gives *Onedin Line* fans an insight into the complexities of making a television series which often had to combine modern technology with the ancient laws of wind and tide.

I am most grateful to everyone who helped in the preparation of this book, to the writers, actors and production staff of the series for generously giving their time and information, and to the BBC for its co-operation. In particular I would like to thank Robin Cecil-Wright, Jean Smith, Archivist of Liverpool Central Library, the Maritime History Department of Merseyside County Museums, John Player and Sons Ltd and the Royal Danish Ministry of Foreign Affairs for assistance with photographic material, *The Sunday Times* and Hugh Johnson for permission to quote from 'One Man's Week', and above all, Captain James Mackreth for his unstinted advice and encouragement.

I should add that this book would not have been written without the somewhat erratic help of one tough old lady—*Charlotte Rhodes*.

Part One
THE ONEDIN STORY

Onedin author Cyril Abraham at work

1 Start of a series

In spite of all the blunt, irascible James Onedin might say, the real founder of the Onedin Line Shipping Company is a cheerful Liverpudlian who now lives well away from the sea in the wooded countryside of Cheshire. Writer Cyril Abraham was involved in research for a new television series eight years ago when the idea of the *Onedin Line* first occurred to him. His original plan had been for a series about a modern shipping company with its boardroom battles and seagoing adventures, but as he went further into the subject he was disappointed to find that almost every big shipping concern was now a conglomerate run by anonymous executives, with no indentifiable personality at the helm.

One thing these British companies had in common was their origin in the bustling commercial years of the mid-nineteenth century. With one or two exceptions each firm was started by a shrewd, far-sighted man who made his name in the business world and with a combination of luck, cunning and ruthlessness built up a shipping empire from modest beginnings.

Third or fourth generation executives often claim to recognise grandfathers or uncles in the Onedin family, but Cyril Abraham insists that the wily James Onedin is the archetypal Victorian shipowner, not modelled on any living figure but drawn in part from all these ambitious, single-minded men.

Abraham himself is no stranger to the sea. As a boy he served aboard the training ship *Conway* before going to sea as an apprentice with the Liverpool shipping line of Lambert and Holt. In all, he spent thirteen years in the

Peter Gilmore as James Onedin

Merchant Navy, some of it before the mast as an able seaman, travelling to ports all over the world with different kinds of cargo and storing up vital first-hand knowledge of harbours and seaways.

Abraham now admits that in common with most sailors who finally 'swallow the anchor' the sea still holds a powerful fascination for him. His first two attempts to give up a sea-faring life were dismal failures, and the third only succeeded, he says, when he threw his discharge book into the fire to make sure he could never go back to sea.

Nowadays he confines his interest to writing about ships and the men who own and work in them, although from time to time he finds himself afloat again during filming sessions for *The Onedin Line*.

The first time he sailed under the BBC flag was during the making of the pilot programme which later became the first episode of the new series; *Charlotte Rhodes*, prepared at breakneck speed to keep up with the filming schedule, was under full sail for the first time since her renovation. In spite of the near-gale which was blowing, the schooner put to sea with members of the film unit, a handful of actors, and the vessel's own crew, dressed for the occasion in Victorian costume.

While the ship headed for a spot designated by the producer, Cyril Abraham chatted with members of *Charlotte*'s crew and discovered uneasily that he was almost the only professional seaman aboard. The vessel was manned by a publican, a biochemist, and only one sailor; even the sailor turned out to be a naval radar operator who spent most of his time watching blips on a darkened screen!

At the wheel he spotted Captain Mackreth, complete with his usual large cigar. 'Is that the skipper?' he asked producer Tony Coburn. 'How much sailing experience does he have?'

'Oh, he's all right,' Coburn assured him. 'He knows the ropes—he used to be a pilot.'

Relieved to discover at least one expert on

Captain Mackreth, in Victorian seaman's costume, takes his vessel out to sea

board, Abraham made his way confidently up the steps to the poop. After all, a river pilot should know all there was to know about wind and tide and the handling of a ship.

'I hear you were a pilot, Captain,' he said conversationally. 'Where was that?'

Captain Mac looked at him briefly, and then nodded at the clouds scudding overhead. 'BEA,' he said.

The same siren song of the sea which lures people from utterly shore-bound professions to sign on as crew aboard *Charlotte Rhodes* has also helped to made the stories of the *Onedin Line* popular all over the world. Letters arrive every day for the author from fans in many different countries, occasionally bearing gifts; one *Onedin* devotee in Canada was heartbroken to discover that every copy of the particular book he wanted had been sold before he could buy one—would the author please supply the missing volume, and would

he accept a copy of *How to Catch Crabs* in return?

The fascination of *The Onedin Line*, says its creator, lies in its nearness to our own times. The late nineteenth century is just beyond the living memory of most people, the days of grandparents and great-uncles, of horse-omnibuses, gaslight and the widowed Queen. It's far enough in the past to be 'different' but not so distant that characters like the forceful

(Right) Brian Rawlinson as Robert Onedin, James' ambitious brother

(Below right) Jessica Benton as Elizabeth Frazer sheds a few untypical tears. Elizabeth was determined to show her brother that a woman could run a shipping line as successfully as any man

(Below) a mock Victorian group pose on the *Charlotte Rhodes*

James or his pompous brother Robert become unrecognisable.

Sheer cussedness, says Cyril Abraham, will keep James Onedin alive to the ripe old age of 102, while his sister Elizabeth will still contrive to have her own way at ninety. He sees them one day as two wizened old autocrats trundling around in wheelchairs, determined not to lose their hold on the shipping business for an instant and making life increasingly difficult for younger members of the family.

Another man James Onedin should thank for his international fame is television producer Peter Graham-Scott, who masterminded the first three series of *The Onedin Line*. The Onedins first appeared on the television screen in a pilot programme produced by Tony Coburn and directed by Bill Slater, and when Peter Graham-Scott inherited the family and their shipping line his first task was to convince the BBC that the story could be translated into a series on a manageable budget. *The Onedin Line* is inevitably a costly series to make; the producer's first consideration was to make sure it didn't become an expensive disaster.

With many years' television production experience behind him Graham-Scott realised that his top priority was a stock of good 'sailing' film—shots of schooners and square-riggers at sea in all kinds of weather, setting sail, tacking, wearing ship, reefing sails, dropping an anchor and any kind of manoeuvre which was part of the normal life of a ship at sea.

In addition to this he wanted film of ships in trouble, taking in sail in a sudden squall, hove-to in raging seas or caught with sails aback. Fortunately, in Captain Mackreth of the schooner *Charlotte Rhodes* and Captain Hansen of the Danish sail-training ship *Danmark* he found two men who became fascinated by the processes involved in

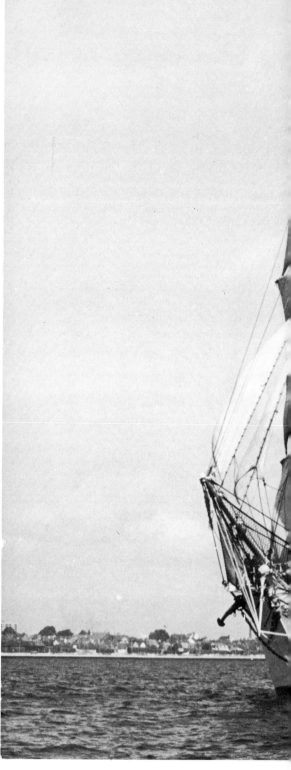

(*Right*) the Danish sail-training ship *Danmark*, seen in several episodes of *The Onedin Line*

Peter Graham-Scott, producer of the first three *Onedin* series, quite at home on the schooner's deck

capturing their vessels on film, and expert in providing the kind of shots which carry television audiences straight back to the days of sail.

To get his library of film Graham-Scott put his camera into a helicopter to swoop down on *Charlotte Rhodes* as she ploughed through the waves under full sail, and went off to the Azores to intercept the *Danmark* whose crew happily donned period costume and leaped up and down the rigging at the director's signal. For the second series the film unit went off to the Virgin Islands to film *Danmark* on her way to the Caribbean, and were lucky enough to find her pitted against the mountainous seas of a bad storm, just the sort of pictures television viewers were to re-member as an integral part of the programme.

With so much sailing footage already safely in the can, Graham-Scott was able to turn his attention to the presentation of the story itself.

Scenes where the action takes place indoors present few problems. A portion of a vast television studio simply becomes James Onedin's house, a shipping office or Elizabeth's drawing-room as the script requires; even the old Liverpool Exchange or Captain Baines' cabin aboard *Charlotte Rhodes* can be recreated with a little careful subterfuge.

Problems begin to arise when the action moves outside the studio, and this was one of the major considerations when the series was first planned. The ideal solution would have been to film in the old docks in Liverpool, now disused and largely silted up, but when the producer went there to have a look at them he decided regretfully that there was too much noise from the busy road nearby and from other modern docks still in use.

Albert Dock presents a forlorn picture today. Its high walls of brick warehouses still surround it, casting a cold shadow behind their squat colonnade, but no ships are warped slowly through the decaying lock gates to tie up alongside. The rumble of traffic from the rest of the dock complex filters faintly past the high buildings, but a sad silence hangs over the dock itself. Nearby Salthouse and Canning Docks are just as deserted, their gates wedged permanently open, weeds and grass pushing up between stone flags which once echoed to the sound of running feet and clattering carts.

The graving docks, too, are empty now except for a lining of silt and rubble at the bottom. The capstans which once hauled ships into the basins for refitting are rusted and rotten, their wooden collars splitting off to lie in dusty splinters on the stone cobbles.

And yet, in spite of the air of neglect which has overtaken these old docks, it's not difficult to conjure up long-gone ships and seamen, to fill the sky once more with a tracery of masts and yards and the wharves with casks and barrels and coils of rope.

Unfortunately it proved impossible for the BBC to do this even for filming purposes, and other suitable locations had to be found. Dartmouth turned out to be an ideal spot for filming many scenes for the early episodes; for one thing *Charlotte Rhodes* was based there and didn't have to make her way round the coast to a new location. Equally important was the old quay at Bayard's Cove with its Georgian Customs House dating from 1739, although the BBC had to persuade the Town Council to take away their *No Parking* signs and a very post-Victorian concrete seat. Across the river was Kingswear Quay which could be disguised as Gibraltar, Morocco, Australia, Carolina, Turkey or Suez as the script required, and in Dartmouth itself there was an original market square with numerous narrow alleyways and twisting streets.

Gradually the people of Dartmouth became accustomed to seeing the BBC's big green vans parked in odd corners, or a group of extras in nineteenth-century costume licking ice-cream cones while they waited to be called in front of the camera. Any unexplained

(*Above*) Bayards Cove, Dartmouth, with its Georgian Customs House and cobbled wharf

(*Below*) filming at Bayards Cove, Dartmouth

(*Above*) the same quay and warehouses as seen in *The Onedin Line* series

(*Top left*) *Onedin Line* props stacked in a Dartmouth car park: everything from life-belts to lobster pots

(*Below left*) Exeter Quay at the turn of the century

events like gunshots or the sudden appearance of a pile of fish-creels in the car-park were bound to be connected with the 'television people'.

Another important location, used in 1971 and again in 1976, was the Old Quay at Exeter which stands on the river at the head of a loop of canal leading from the city to rejoin the River Exe on its way to the sea at Exmouth. The quay gave the production unit a length of handsome nineteenth-century waterfront complete with mellow stone and brick warehouses uninterrupted by modern shop-fronts or sign-boards. Equally important was the non-tidal water alongside. Since filming a scene which only occupies minutes on a television screen may take several hours of the unit's time, ships tied up at a tidal wharf will rise and fall with the tide, ending up at a different level in each shot; one minute viewers might see most of the bulwarks, the next minute very little of the deck at all, and in the final shot only the masts and yards. This makes life very difficult for the production team, but at Exeter it was fortunately no problem.

One tremendous bonus derived from filming at Exeter Quay was the existence in the nearby canal basin of Exeter Maritime Museum with its excellent collection of craft from all over the world. Many of these were borrowed for episodes in the series, either as actual vessels involved in the story or as authentic 'dressing' for port scenes.

One of the museum's proudest possessions is a dock dredger designed by Isambard Kingdom Brunel and built in 1844—the oldest working steam-propelled boat in the world. Known affectionately as *Bertha*, the little dredger's boiler room and thundering steam engine were featured on film at various times, with a high-prowed Portuguese Tagus lighter which made its television debut under sail as a coaler in the 'Cape Verde Islands'.

The museum has not only supplied craft ranging from an East African dug-out canoe to a boat full of Arab raiders, but on occasion has even provided the Arabs as well, not to mention longshoremen, Cape Verde coal hawkers and odd surly groups coming under the general description of 'layabouts'.

In spite of the obvious advantages of Exeter Quay there were inevitably one or two problems to be sorted out before filming could start. Although traffic noise was minimal and no planes roared overhead or trains rattled past, a new motorway was under construction nearby and pile-drivers hammered all day building bridges over the Exe. From time to time a message was sent to the site to ask for work to be suspended for a few minutes while dialogue was recorded, since the sensitive sound equipment would pick up any stray twentieth-century noises.

The motorway was to prove a far greater obstacle several years later, but during these first episodes it was only necessary to arrange for some extra dredging work to be done in the canal so that *Charlotte Rhodes* and the smaller *Provident* could make their way up to the quay.

One aspect which worried Peter Graham-Scott was the possibility of losing someone overboard while the vessels were at sea. To

Designers dress the Old Quay at Exeter

make sure everyone knew exactly what they were doing he issued a leaflet to all members of the unit naming the different parts of a sailing ship and explaining how they all functioned; it also contained a stern warning to anyone becoming blasé about moving around on board and starting to take silly risks. Pride goeth before a swim!

Appropriately enough one of the most experienced sailors in the cast is Howard Lang

(*Right*) two views of the gaily-painted Tagus lighter which became a coaler in the Cape Verde Islands for one *Onedin* episode

(*Below right*) the tug *St Canute* berthed outside Exeter Maritime Museum

(*Below*) *Bertha*, the Brunel dredger, with smoke puffing from her funnel

who plays the crusty but kindly Captain Baines. In his spare time he sails a sixteen-foot yacht of his own regularly from Chichester Harbour near the Isle of Wight, and he has retained a great interest in larger ships from his days in the Navy when he became as familiar as the salty Baines with the waters of the Caribbean, the Straits of Malacca and the ports of the Indian Ocean.

While he doesn't relish clinging to the mast with a BBC typhoon of fire-hoses soaking him to the skin, he admits that at least it's safer than the real thing—he was once caught in a landing-craft between Bangkok and Singapore in the storm which inspired Herman Wouk's *Caine Mutiny*, forty-eight hours of wind-lashed seas and towering waves which caused the loss of several ships.

For many people the earnest, weather-wise

Baines is the archetypal Victorian seaman, and regular fans of the series have developed quite an affection for the well-meaning captain. So many visitors to the schooner *Charlotte Rhodes* ask, 'Where's Captain Baines today, then?' that the crew now say with straight faces, 'Oh, he went ashore for a pint about an hour ago, and we haven't seen him since!'

In the same way Howard Lang has found himself hailed affably by complete strangers in the streets of San Francisco and New York, and besieged by appreciative letters from West Germany. On a recent trip to Grimstad in Norway to open a shopping complex some 25,000 people turned out to meet him and it took four policemen several minutes to find him in the crowd. Grimstad has connections with the sea going back far into the past, and there's hardly a family in town without a husband, brother or father at sea and a row of faded portraits of Victorian seamen in the hall.

It would be quite wrong to leave the subject of the series' beginnings without mentioning one aspect which will be remembered as long as the story itself. For most people the sweeping strings of Aram Khachaturian's splendid *Spartacus* adagio immediately conjure up a vision of soaring masts and wind-filled sails or a sharp bow cleaving the sea into foaming ripples along a lean hull. Television viewers who have never seen the ballet for which the

(*Left*) one of the series' most popular characters —Howard Lang as the faithful Baines

(*Top right*) under full sail except for gaff topsails on main and mizzen, *Charlotte Rhodes* heads out to sea with a film crew aboard. Her red sails make her instantly recognisable wherever she goes

(*Below right*) with red sails catching the sun, *Charlotte Rhodes* is the centre of attention

(*Overleaf*) Ken Hutchison as Matt Harvey waits for James Onedin to come alongside

(*Above*) James Onedin and Captain Baines caught in a typhoon on the deck of *Charlotte Rhodes*. The flat sea in the background wasn't evident on the television screen!

(*Left*) the brigantine *Marquès*, complete with false funnel, anchored in the River Dart as the steamer *Prince Edward*

music was written still know the unmistakable strains of the *Onedin Line* theme, and its various recordings have been best-sellers several times.

The version used for the series itself extracts every ounce of theatrical thrill from the music; it's a Decca recording of the Vienna Philharmonic Orchestra conducted by the composer. Since the series has not been seen in Russia, Khachaturian only discovered quite recently that his music had found a new popularity on the television screen, and claims to be thoroughly mystified by the whole business. Sailing ships, he says, couldn't have been further from his mind when the music was composed. Unfortunately, because the Soviet Union is not a signatory to the international copyright agreements, the composer doesn't benefit financially from the thousands of records his work has sold overseas.

The happy inspiration to use the *Spartacus* theme was the combined achievement of producer Peter Graham-Scott and his musical adviser Anthony Isaac. After listening to hours of music by Sibelius the choice was narrowed down to the Khachaturian theme or Sibelius' *Fifth Symphony*, and both men felt that the *Spartacus* music set the right mood for the series.

With painstaking care a film sequence of sailing ships was prepared and the crash of the sea on plunging bows became the first few seconds of each episode, copied in sound by a torrent of strings and the smash of tympani.

(*Left to right*) Howard Lang as Baines, Peter Graham-Scott (producer), Anne Stallybrass as Anne Onedin and Peter Gilmore as James Onedin

2 *Charlotte Rhodes* - A Star is Born

The little Devon town of Dartmouth is a quiet place in late summer. In their hotels the last of the tourists are packing their bags, the pleasure-boats on the river attract fewer customers, and the narrow twisting streets settle back into their customary unhurried peace.

High on the hill behind the town the Britannia Naval College looks serenely out over the Dart Estuary where the blue-green waters once lapped the ships of Raleigh and the Pilgrim Fathers. Across the river the select residences of Kingswear rise in orderly suburban rows up the wooded hillside, over-looking a harbour which sheltered Coeur-de-Lion's crusaders embarking for the Holy Land.

One September evening in 1970, as if to complete this tranquil and timeless scene, the russet sails of a topsail schooner appeared in the entrance to the Narrows. The setting sun gently touched her spars and bulwarks with gold; her raked stem cut cleanly through the dark waves, throwing a gilded ripple back along her bows.

Evidently the ship was coming into harbour under sail, planning to round up into the wind at the precise moment to pick up her moorings. On the esplanade one or two late promenaders paused to watch the rare and awe-inspiring sight of a ship under sail handled with consummate skill by an experienced crew.

But as the schooner raced on into harbour, it began to look as if all was not going according to plan. On the poop her skipper realised to his horror that his crew were not really experienced enough to get the sails down in time; the Lower Ferry hesitated in its methodical crossing as the schooner dashed past with frantic figures scrambling for the topsail yards and tugging wildly at the big fore-and-afters. As usual, the harbour was cluttered with dinghies and yachts bobbing in lines at their moorings, and to leave room for her turn into the wind the schooner had to hug the row of moored boats on the Kings-wear side of the river. Abruptly the skipper put his helm hard over, and with red sails flailing on all sides the vessel turned for the Dartmouth shore. To everyone's dismay the schooner showed no sign of coming to a stop, and as she fled like an arrow towards the line of expensive craft moored on the Dartmouth side, her skipper hastily decided to modify his swash-buckling entrance by starting the engine.

With her throttle wide open and her pro-peller at full pitch the schooner roared off downriver again on a curving track towards the Narrows, far too fast to pick up any of the mooring buoys bobbing in her path. Desper-ately her luckless commander tried to dis-engage the clutch, only managing to trap the hand of one of his crew who was trying to wind the throttle back. There was only one possible course—full astern.

With a tremendous shuddering the schooner's headlong flight slowed and finally halted, and she began to grind ponderously sternwards through the water. But as the vessel picked up speed it was suddenly evident that regardless of the direction steered, astern also meant starboard.

While his moaning assistant tried in vain to

A Devon landmark: *Charlotte Rhodes* moored in the River Dart

(Right) Charlotte Rhodes under full sail

drag his mangled fingers from the clutch controls, the skipper glanced, horrified, over the stern of his ship. Right in her backwards path was a magnificent 90ft 'gin-palace', a confection in glittering white with shiny brass rails and varnished teak trim. Agonised, he waited for the crash which would herald a £150,000 insurance claim.

The crash never came. The schooner cleared the yacht's stern by inches and vanished on her hectic sternwards course up the river.

The gulls had long since settled back on the river buoys when some time later the schooner returned at a more stately pace and tied up at her moorings for the night. Slowly peace descended on the river of Raleigh and the Pilgrim Fathers. *Charlotte Rhodes* was back again from her first week under sail.

Just in case anyone imagines it's an easy matter to manoeuvre a 130ft schooner in crowded waters, a glance at any book written about the days of the old coasting vessels would soon prove otherwise. Some pages of these memoirs are a catalogue of collisions and near-misses, and that was before the days of dinghy helmsmen who insist on smacking

their craft into the solid bows of schooners on their way up narrow channels, howling indignantly, 'Can't you see I'm *racing*?'

The close attentions of small boats have dogged *Charlotte Rhodes* ever since she became involved with the *Onedin Line* series. Trawlers veer off course to inspect her, coasters edge over for a better look and tiny racing yachts dart under her bow so that their crews can take photographs.

Charlotte, like the dignified elderly lady she is, takes all this adulation in her measured stride as the respect due to a vessel of such advanced years. Fame has come to her late in life—nine years ago she was just another Danish merchant vessel ferrying cargoes of building materials across the Skagerrak, her one stumpy mast a glorified derrick to hoist bulging sacks out of her hold.

Charlotte Rhodes began life in 1904 in a shipyard in Svendborg on the island of Fünen. Built as a three-masted schooner she battled with the North Atlantic gales for many years under sail alone, carrying general cargo from Denmark to North America and Canada and returning with a hold full of salt cod.

In those days she was called the *Eva*, 130ft from taffrail to jib-boom, with a beam of 22ft and a draught of 8ft 6in at her stern. Unlike most Baltic schooners her semi-elliptical counter stern is combined with a steeply raked stem and the sharp underwater lines of a clipper. Even equipped with a diesel engine and more or less dismasted she still looked a vessel of fine sailing qualities.

In 1968 Captain James Mackreth was just about to land his last BEA Trident at Heathrow Airport and retire from commercial flying for good. His airborne career had spanned planes of all kinds, from Bristol fighters to modern jets, and his spare time was spent pursuing speed on the ground, in the shape of a racing Lister Jaguar. Not a man to put his feet up by the fire when he gave up flying, Captain Mackreth began to look round for a new project to keep himself occupied.

During off-duty hours on his last few trips to Denmark he started to inspect some of the old trading vessels which were up for sale, never finding one which entirely satisfied him. One morning he took the ferry across the Lim Fjord in the north of Denmark to the little island of Für near Ålborg to look at yet another ship, a former schooner called the *Meta Jan*. The harbour turned out to be tiny, entirely filled by the three vessels tied up there. Two of them were nondescript and uninteresting, and of the third all that could be seen as the ferry neared the island was a graceful stem and a long bowsprit projecting

beyond one of the buildings on the wharf.

The *Meta Jan* turned out to be this mysterious third ship, the vessel which had started life as the *Eva* sixty-four years before. Already a venerable age for a wooden schooner, her lines still showed their elegant sweep in spite of a jumble of ramshackle deck-houses which had been added over the years. Captain Mackreth immediately fell for the old ship and agreed to buy her subject to a satisfactory report on her condition.

It was obvious from the start that her name would have to be changed. English pronunciation would turn *Meta Jan* into the dreadful 'Meaty Ann', and the Mackreth family began to search for a suitable alternative. Yacht names were no use for such a gracious old lady—to christen her 'Hellzapoppin' or 'Little Mermaid' would have been unthinkable.

A list of comparable British schooners at the turn of the century reads like the roll-call of a select ladies' seminary—*Margaret Ann, Elizabeth Ellen Fisher, Maggie Kelso, Sarah Latham*—the names of wives, sisters and daughters of the men who owned and sailed these ships. Captain Mackreth decided to follow tradition, and renamed his new ship after his wife's great-great-grandmother, Charlotte Rhodes, a lady of great character who shocked her family by eloping with her father's groom.

The length of this new name was to cause problems when the schooner eventually landed the part of James Onedin's first ship. The BBC's original script concerned a vessel called the *Anne*, and for filming purposes the name was to be painted prominently on the ship's side. By this time magnificent new name-boards had been fixed to the schooner's bows, specially carved in a Danish shipyard with the name *Charlotte Rhodes* in square old-fashioned lettering, and understandably Captain Mackreth was reluctant to take them off again.

After much head-scratching the BBC property men decided there was no successful way of disguising such a long name behind boards reading *Anne*, and the matter was referred back to the producer. In the end he

relented and *Charlotte Rhodes* came into the story as the first ship of the Onedin Line, name-boards and all.

The graceful schooner whose three-masted silhouette was to become so familiar to television viewers was still very much in the future when she arrived for the first time at her new home in Dartmouth. She had been fitted with new masts before leaving Denmark

but her stern was disfigured by a vast deck-house on three levels which contained galley, chartroom and wheelhouse. The people of Dartmouth promptly christened the old ship 'The Three Chicken-Houses', and waited to see what would happen to her.

For the next two years Captain Mackreth—'Captain Mac' as he became known to the BBC film unit—worked on his ship in all

A more recent picture than it looks at first sight—*Charlotte Rhodes* in a Hull drydock in 1976

weathers, clearing away the ugly deckhouses which spoiled her lines, drawing out sail-plans, splicing wire rope for standing rigging and manilla for the halliards and sheets, shaping tree-trunks for gaffs and booms to take his sails, and reeving the numerous heavy wooden blocks which constitute the 'machinery' of a sailing craft. On board he found some of the gear which had been used in the schooner's sailing days decades before, dragged it out into the daylight and put it back to work. Belaying-pins went back into the pin-rails and rigging-screws into the standing gear. Later on a wooden wheel was added on the poop, and on the mizzen boom-gallows a shiny brass bell appeared bearing the inscription *Charlotte Rhodes*.

Below decks the long hold was divided in two at the base of the mainmast. The after section eventually became a saloon with bench seats round the sides, while the forward area was left just as it had been, an open hold. Between these two sections went a little galley with calor-gas cookers and a double steel sink. Right in the bow was a small forecastle with five bunks and a wooden ladder leading up to the deck above. As a sign of changing times some Danish official had carved on its cross-beam 'Crew space for two seamen', as many of a crew as the little coaster had needed.

Visitors familiar with *Charlotte Rhodes* from her television appearances often ask to see the spacious, panelled cabin under the poop where Captain Baines holds court. Alas, that fine cabin only exists on the floor of a tele-vision studio, not aboard a sailing ship. Probably at the time when the schooner sailed without an engine a cabin of a similar type but more modest dimensions would have extended the length of the poop. Nowadays half that space is taken up by the 210hp Rolls-Royce diesel engine, generators for electricity and—the ultimate sacrilege—a central heating unit. This leaves just enough room under the poop for a small and strictly utilitarian cabin in the stern which also doubles as a chart-room, housing the radar unit, radio, electronic log, direction-finding gear and an echo-sounder. As Captain Baines might say, 'I

(*Above and right*) *Charlotte Rhodes* in the Irish Sea

dunno, Mister Onedin, but it all looks like new-fangled nonsense to me . . .'

One of the most useful new-fangled additions has been the Rolls-Royce engine, substituted for the more unreliable Grenaa which caused so much bother during the flying entrance to Dartmouth Harbour. Now, with the aid of tides and currents, *Charlotte* can be manoeuvred successfully in even the most restricted waters.

In spite of the engine her main source of propulsion is 3,500 sq ft of terylene divided into eleven separate sails on her three masts. Rigged as a topsail schooner, in addition to a big fore-and-aft sail on each mast, gaff topsails on main and mizzen, a staysail and three jibs, she carries two square topsails on her fore-mast. Many of the old British coasting schooners did away with these square sails,

since in spite of the extra speed they can provide in the right wind conditions, it's a risky and time-consuming job to go out on the yards to set or stow them.

As an airline pilot Captain Mackreth was also a qualified navigator. With indefatigable enthusiasm he added the Board of Trade Ocean-going Yachtmaster's Certificate, a radar qualification, a radio operator's ticket, and—shades of the old days—a certificate in First Aid at Sea. Fortunately the most serious injury he's had to treat so far is a broken toe!

As luck would have it, renovation work on *Charlotte* was nearly complete when the BBC started their search for a suitable vessel to film the *Onedin Line* series. Of all the ships undergoing reconstruction *Charlotte Rhodes* was the nearest to completion, with only a suit of sails to find. After several weeks of concerted effort Captain Mac had his ship ready on the appointed day, the first time he had ever seen her under full sail.

Like any old lady *Charlotte Rhodes* has her

difficult moments, but she can also turn on considerable charm. When not performing for the cameras she earns her keep in private charter work, posing for advertising photographs, taking part in television commercials or acting as a gracious hostess on promotional tours.

Considering that at heart she's an Edwardian lady, one or two of these charters must have given her rather a surprise, and one in particular probably shocked her to the core. The advertising agency in question had decided to feature the schooner in a lavish calendar promoting a well known brand of rum; the pictures were to be the 'log' of an idyllic South-Sea voyage through palm-fringed lagoons and coral islands, where clear blue waters foam on silver shores.

Unfortunately for *Charlotte*'s crew the budget didn't run to real coral islands, and photography was scheduled for three days in the Dart Estuary. Luckily the first day turned out to be hot and sunny, and the schooner, with a trio of svelte models aboard, sailed out past Dartmouth Castle to drop anchor off Start Point.

As everyone bustled about clearing the decks so that work could begin, the photographer had a swift conference with his models and made his way over to the main-mast where the crew were furling the sail.

'It would be a great help,' he began confidentially, 'if you could all move forward to the bow while we take the pictures. Would you mind?'

'Oh, don't worry about us,' they assured him, 'we often have picture-sessions aboard *Charlotte Rhodes*. Just you go ahead, and we'll keep out of your way.'

'Well, that's not really the problem,' explained the photographer apologetically. 'You see the girls are a little—well—nervous . . .'

Bashful photographic models? This unusual notion had everyone puzzled until the first girl appeared at the wheel. She wore two copper bracelets, a narrow strip of brown material round her hips, and a rather apprehensive smile. Apparently the calendar was to

be a sea-going Pirelli, with a crew of topless tars.

After a couple of trial shots the photographer decided the light was too strong for the mellow skin-tones he had in mind and abandoned the photo-session until later. The models yawned resignedly and stretched themselves out on the hatchcovers to sunbathe.

By the time lighting conditions were suitable again the girls had decided to get an all-over tan, and had discarded even their copper bracelets.

Later that evening the story of *Charlotte Rhodes* and her crew of naked models spread rapidly round the pubs of Dartmouth. As the schooner prepared to leave for her next day's work there was a queue on the quay waiting to sign on.

To most people, though, the real attraction is the ship herself, and wherever she ties up in port little knots of people gather to watch the activity on board. There's a scramble to catch the heaving-line and drop the thick polypropelene warps over the nearest bollards; engineers in oily overalls stroll along from nearby freighters and rig supply ships; fathers point out details of the rigging to their small sons, and elderly men recall the days when it was possible to walk right across the harbour on the decks of anchored sailing-ships.

'She's smaller than I thought.'

'Where's the crow's nest, mister? Where's the guns?'

'Wouldn't like to be in her in a storm.'

'Oh, I don't know—she must have an engine of some kind, the sails'll just be for show.'

'Can we climb the rigging, mister? *Please* can we?'

Perhaps the question which annoys Captain Mackreth most of all is 'How did you get her here?' as if the least possible means of locomotion was *sail*. To anyone who has seen *Charlotte* romping through a Force-8 gale or tugging at her moorings, anxious to get to sea again, it seems incredible that people should consider her a museum-piece. When she was dry-docked recently in Hull the frames between the double skin of planking were found to be as sound as the day she was built, a tribute to the craftsmen of seventy years ago.

One of *Charlotte*'s less endearing little ways is a determination to stay in the age of sail and reject all modern mechanical devices. Among these, unfortunately, she numbers taps and pumps as well as more complex items like radar and the generators. For no apparent reason mysterious faults develop, plunging everyone aboard back into the world of Onedin with hissing oil-lamps and the steady 'thump-splosh' of a back-breaking bilge-pump.

Charlotte seems to enjoy these excursions into the past, reliving the times of her Atlantic voyages when the smell of the salt sea was unmixed with diesel fumes, and the clatter of her rigging-blocks and the creak of her timbers were the loudest noises on board. Even her crew derive a great satisfaction from being able to sail the old ship as their fore-fathers might have done, out in the timeless sea, far beyond the reach of telephone or transistor radio, where the wind and the tides are the most important things in life.

But the responsibility of keeping an old wooden ship at sea is considerable. Every year she has to be taken out of the water, her hull cleaned and inspected and re-painted with an anti-fouling compound. Any soft wood is cut out and replaced, and caulking renewed where necessary. Above the water-line there is always work to be done; deck seams must be caulked to keep out seas breaking over the bulwarks, manilla halliards and sheets must be renewed, the engine and generators overhauled, mast-wedges cut, rigging-blocks oiled, masts greased, odd planks replaced here and there and a thousand and one other tasks.

Charlotte Rhodes in the North Channel, 1975

In the past, to save the cost of shipyard labour, Captain Mackreth did much of this skilled and time-consuming work himself, financing inescapable slipway charges from the schooner's own earnings. It was an exhausting way of life, and some months ago he decided regretfully to pass on to someone else the task of keeping *Charlotte Rhodes* in sea-going condition and at the same time finding work for her to do.

Charlotte's winning ways had charmed a Dutch businessman, John ter Haak, who runs a marina and a yacht importing firm in Amsterdam, and on 1 November 1976 she entered the Noord Zee Kanaal which links Amsterdam with the North Sea, exactly a hundred years after it was first opened. She was on her way to a new home at ter Haak's marina near Amsterdam among the cabin-cruisers and sleek modern yachts, where her new owner proposes to undertake more restoration work in her holds.

Ter Haak is no stranger to film work—he was one of the power-boat drivers in the film *Puppet on a Chain*—and he's anxious for *Charlotte Rhodes* to continue her television career whenever possible. What the future holds for the old schooner, no one can tell.

Part Two
SETTING FOR A SERIES

3 Crews, Crimps and Coffin-Ships

One of the principal reasons for the great international success of *The Onedin Line* must be the authentic picture which it presents of life at sea in the late nineteenth century. The seafaring adventures of the Onedin family and their rivals represent many hours of painstaking research on the part of author Cyril Abraham and members of the production team into the lives of seamen ashore and aboard ship; sailors' clothing, and equipment, contemporary navigational skills, cargoes carried, intricacies of rigging, ports of call, freight rates, the location of steam coaling-stations, methods of cargo handling—all these

matters and a hundred others must be investigated to provide the accurate background detail of each story.

Paradoxically, it was the prosaic steamship which finally removed much of the hardship and danger from the seamen's lives, improving living and working conditions beyond anything which a sailing ship could offer. Aboard the beautiful tall ships, in sharp contrast to their stately grace, the lives of the seamen could be hard and squalid; short hours of sleep, snatched fully clad in wet oilskins on a bunk already damp with sea-water, could make a man old before his time,

(*Above*) the Norwegian barque *Gunvor* photographed just before she broke up on the Lizard in 1913

(*Left*) Dartmouth in 1886. The brigs of the Naval training fleet are surrounded by schooners, ketches and a pair of steam yachts in the foreground

and yet the crews of these ships took a fierce pride in their calling. The 'stinking steam-kettles' might drive sail from the seas, but they would never command the same grim loyalty as the tall ships.

There's an old sea superstition that a child born with a 'caul', or membrane, round his head will never drown. In seafaring communities a caul would be dried and preserved for the day when the boy would go to sea, taking it with him wherever he sailed as a charm against the dangers of storm and shipwreck.

How effective this really was, no one will ever know, but certainly some kind of magic was necessary if a man was to survive for long in what a century ago was still a very perilous profession.

Between 1850 and 1865 nearly 20,000 ships were lost at sea and incalculable numbers of seamen drowned or cast adrift in small boats to die of exposure. Numerous accidents could cause the wreck of a ship—a combination of wind and tide, being caught on a lee shore by a change of wind, uncharted rocks, a shifting cargo, dismasting, collision with another ship or an iceberg—all these misfortunes could overtake even a well run vessel.

In some ships, however, there were additional dangers: an incompetent or drunken master, slack discipline, lack of proper maintenance, and penny-pinching on the part of owners quite prepared to send out an unseaworthy vessel with an overloaded hold.

To keep a ship in good running order it had to be dry-docked regularly and its hull cleaned and inspected. If it was a wooden ship soft planking had to be cut away and replaced, and caulking renewed. If the hull was iron it had to be inspected for strained rivets and areas of rust. Every rope had to be renewed regularly and standing rigging replaced, ready to take the strain of a sudden bad storm.

Inevitably this all cost money and reduced the profit from each of the vessel's voyages. Parsimonious owners insisted that every

fathom of rope and every pot of paint be accounted for, and grumbled dismally about each extra day the ship was held up in port. All too often dangerous defects showed up for the first time in the towering seas off Cape Horn when topmasts and yards carried away or strained rivets finally sprang loose, letting icy water burst into the hold.

Unscrupulous masters also found ways of making some money out of the ship's transactions. A friendly chandler might hand out gifts in return for regular trade, or the crew's rations could be cut to the minimum and the owner sent a bill for the full amount. Some masters made the most of their 'slop chests' by ensuring that the crew couldn't find so much as a spare inch of thread on board without buying it at exorbitant prices.

Another dangerous short-cut was to under-ballast an empty ship while charging the owner for the proper amount. As a result the

(*Left*) with her lower yards cockbilled, the tea clipper *Titania* undergoes repair work to her stem in drydock

Liverpool's Langton Graving Docks in the 1890s, with the sailing ship *Baring Brothers* in No. 4 Compartment

vessel wasn't stiff enough to maintain a proper
balance in heavy seas, and the master counted
on good weather to get him to his next port of
call. A favourite place for this trick was the
notorious West Coast, the guano islands and
nitrate ports of South America, where many
under-ballasted ships disappeared in sudden
unexpected storms.

Conversely, in pursuit of profit many owners
tried to overload their ships well past the
point of safety. With hardly any freeboard
these vessels were at the mercy of the sea,
unable to rise to meet oncoming waves which
swamped them and drove them under.

In January 1865 the 1752-ton auxiliary
steamer *London* was lost 200 miles south of
Land's End on her way to Australia. To the
bottom with her she took 200 passengers and
crew, and though the subsequent enquiry
held no-one to blame the suggestion was made
that she had been seriously overloaded.

Appropriately enough it was James Hall,
himself a Tyneside shipowner, who made the
first move to prevent overloaded ships putting
to sea. In a letter to *The Times* he told the
story of a ship lost on her way to Shanghai
with coal. Before she left port the hull was
leaking so badly that the pumps could hardly
keep the water-level from rising. In spite of
this her owner allowed her to sail, and three
days later the ship sank at sea, her crew
fortunately saved by another vessel.

Hall's fellow shipowners protested vigor-
ously. How could Britain maintain her world
trade, they wanted to know, if she loaded less
into her ships than foreign competitors? Hall
was adamant—the lives of seamen were more
important than an impressive balance-sheet.

There was another and more sinister reason
for the shipowners' readiness to risk their
vessels. If a ship was wrecked at sea the under-
writers paid the vessel's value in full plus the
cost of its cargo. Once a ship had passed its

best and begun to require extensive repairs it was of little interest to the owner whether it stayed afloat for many years or became a wreck, particularly if it was over-insured. In the days of wooden hulls it wasn't unknown for an owner to hire a 'wrecker', a man who signed on as a member of the crew and deliberately sabotaged the ship in a seaway where he knew he was likely to be rescued.

The man whose name is best known in connection with loading legislation is Samuel Plimsoll who championed Hall's cause in the House of Commons. In 1871 a law was passed requiring the compulsory marking of depth guages on stem and stern and the recording of a ship's draught when it sailed, but there was still no restriction on what that draught ought to be. Under certain conditions seamen could demand a survey if they thought their ship was unseaworthy or overloaded but this legislation was virtually unworkable in practice. A shipowner with a squad of police at his back could soon persuade a reluctant crew to

drop their objections—sometimes with tragic results.

It wasn't until 1890 that the Board of Trade had the authority to mark a load-line and a circle on each vessel's side to indicate the water-line at maximum freight.

In spite of their reluctance to impose loading restrictions on British vessels the Government did achieve one important reform in 1873. After a collision at sea the master of any ship involved was obliged by law to stand by to give assistance to the other vessel; this made it absolutely illegal for him to dash away in the hope of remaining anonymous, although it didn't always prevent a captain from trying to do so.

Certain areas of the seas are particularly dangerous because of congestion and the resulting high risk of collision. The Straits of Dover were (and still are) a maritime bottle-neck of vast proportions, but in the days of sail the problem of beating to windward could add another dimension to the problem of dodging shipping in this narrow waterway. As the days of the steam engine advanced, many sailing ships were mown down by steamers whose bridge officers had either forgotten or were too young to know how a square-rigger manoeuvred.

It was a disaster like this which overtook the beautiful little barque *Berean*, a composite iron and wood ship built in 1869 by Pile of Sunderland. Only 160ft long, her mainmast was 116ft from deck to truck, her quarterdeck planked with knotless New Zealand pine and her bulwarks decorated with fretwork panels. In addition her deck-housing, forecastle panelling, fife rails and even her lifeboats were all of polished teak.

For many years *Berean* seemed to bear a charmed life, avoiding the accidents which sooner or later overtook most sailing ships of her time. However, in 1910, after fourteen years spent in the tough business of ferrying Norwegian ice to London, she collided with a steamer and ended up as a hulk off Falmouth in Cornwall.

Perhaps the most famous incident of this kind is the sinking of the *Northfleet*. Built on the Thames in 1853, the *Northfleet* had seen twenty years of faithful service carrying passengers and troops to the Black Sea and the Far East by the time she was put into the emigrant trade. One day in January 1873 she was riding out a storm near Dungeness when a mystery steamer collided with her bow and made off, leaving the *Northfleet* to sink in twenty minutes, taking with her some 300 emigrants.

The guilty steamer was the Spanish ship *Murillo*. Although her master immediately tried to disguise his damaged bow with a coat of paint the vessel was still badly scarred and was soon identified as the missing hit-and-run ship. After this tragedy every British ship was required to display its name clearly on each bow and again at the stern.

Unlike so many of the masters in sail, there was no guarantee that the captain of a steamer had many years' sea-going experience. In the early 1870s he might well be twenty-two years old, with the ink barely dry on his master's certificate. For a monthly salary of £15 to £25 depending on where his ship was bound he was in sole command of the vessel, her crew and provisions—three shillings a day for each officer and one-and-ninepence for sailors and firemen (stokers).

While Parliament continued the lengthy debate on making ships safer at sea the laws relating to the feeding, payment and housing of crews and the proper certification of masters were also brought up to date. In 1880 the Seamen's Wages Bill took the major step of abolishing the advance note, one of the most exploited institutions in the history of seafaring.

The idea behind an advance on wages was sound enough; a shipowner allowed a prospective employee a certain sum—usually his first month's wages—in advance of sailing, in order to buy anything he might need for the coming voyage. This sum was given in the form of an advance note, a draft which could be cashed ten days after the ship had sailed, and it was given to a seaman after he had signed the articles of agreement in front of the ship's captain.

All too often the note was cashed immediately by a boarding-house master, the proprietor of some dingy hovel near the waterfront where a sailor had found a bed for the night. If the man didn't join his ship at sailing-time the note would be worthless, so the boarding-house master awarded himself a large discount just in case. This discount usually amounted to 25 or 30 per cent of the face value, compared with the 5 per cent charged by a sailors' home.

Often a returning seaman would fall into the hands of a 'crimp', a dockland entrepreneur who specialised in finding beds for sailors, crews for ships, and anything else for which someone was prepared to pay. The crimp would take his victim to taverns, brothels and gaming-houses, buying him fancy shore-going clothes on credit and collecting a commission on everything as he went. Eventually the seaman would be presented with a colossal

bill, and—suddenly sober and repentant—would have to sign on for another voyage in order to draw an advance on his wages to pay what he owed the crimp. For finding him this new berth the crimp would charge an additional £1; a sailors' home would have made the arrangements for one-and-sixpence.

From time to time men were 'shanghaied'—picked up in some low dive by a crimp, drugged and ferried out to a waiting ship which needed more men for its crew. The unfortunate victim, who might not even have been a seaman in the first place, woke up with a sore head in some unknown forecastle on its way down the Channel, penniless and without a pair of seaboots or a few rags to his name. It might be two years before he saw Britain again.

Bad though this practice became in British ports, it never existed on such a scale as in San Francisco, where the notorious 'Barbary Coast' was a lawless den of drinking, fighting, gambling and whoring; in its hey-day hundreds of men were taken unconscious to ships waiting in the harbour, and no captain

The little *Berean*, dwarfed by bigger vessels in Oslo harbour

could recruit a crew without buying the help of the crimps.

Police who were forced to enter this area of San Francisco carried weighted clubs and a version of an early Bowie knife nearly a foot long. Sailors going ashore there found Chinese tattoo shops where they could have hearts, stars and sweethearts' names applied to their arms, a fiery dragon coiled between their shoulder-blades or a portrait of their ship under full sail across chest and stomach. Good teeth were sometimes removed to make room for gold at Henry Cogswell's 'Painless Dental Parlour'; in Jackson Street a sailor could have the Chinese girl of his choice for 25 cents—'China girl nice! You come inside, please?' adding for some unfathomable reason, 'Your father, he just go out!'

If a seaman wanted a drink he could visit the Bull Run, the Dew Drop Inn, the Montana, the Coliseum or the Billy Goat cellar in Kearny Street where the Irish proprietrix, Pigeon-Toed Sal, kept order with a derringer and a hickory wagon-spoke. In any of these dives a likely-looking sailor was liable to be served with a knock-out potion and shipped off to the harbour by notorious crimps like 'Jimmy the Drummer' who was once said to have foisted a corpse on a luckless captain. Since his potential 'crew' were all limp carcases anyway, the cunning Jimmy also collected a fee for the one which was not only limp, but cold.

Many shipmasters encouraged their crews to desert in San Francisco. At the time, the wages of deserting seamen reverted to the master and the owners, and since the men weren't needed while the ship discharged a cargo or waited for a new one, their absence also saved money. By getting in touch with the right people a master could easily arrange for a new crew to 'sign on' when he was ready to sail again.

But the vice dens of San Francisco had their staunch opponents. The Reverend James Fell—'Fell of Frisco'—claimed to have beaten up every crimp on the Barbary Coast. In British ports the chaplains of the Missions to Seamen made valiant and often successful attempts to stop the spread of crimping. At one time crimps' runners, sometimes twenty or thirty at a time, would board a ship as she came into port, daring the officers to prevent them, and take off the men and their baggage then and there. Eventually the Reverend R. B. Boyer complained to the Board of Trade and squads of police were detailed to meet incoming ships.

The chaplains also waited in the shipping offices as crews were paid off, suggesting to them that money should be sent home immediately to their wives and families. One enterprising clergyman eventually commissioned a fleet of cabs to wait outside the shipping office in order to rush paid-off seamen to the railway station before the crimps could lay hands on them.

By this time seamen were beginning to organise themselves into unions in an effort to improve their own conditions of pay and service. In 1878 a union was formed in Sunderland with a shilling entrance fee and a weekly due of threepence. One of its members, Joseph Havelock Wilson, pressed strongly for a national organisation, and some nine years later representatives of the small local groups in ports all round the country met in Sunderland to form the National Amalgamated Sailors' and Firemen's Union of Great Britain and Ireland. By 1889 Samuel Plimsoll was President and the union claimed 40,000 members in thirty-six branches.

It would be wrong to give the impression that every ship in the later nineteenth century was a badly run, dangerous hulk where callous officers bullied their drunken crew into resentful obedience. Many undoubtedly were, but others were vessels of inspired design and grace whose owners and crews took a pride in them. Aboard these ships the crews were competent, hard-working seamen who went about their duties with skill and courage in conditions which, although still hard, were as comfortable as circumstances would allow.

During their spare time in port or in the calms of the Doldrums these men produced

Captain Thomas (*back row, centre*) and the crew of the four-masted barque *Afon Alaw* at San Francisco, at the turn of the century. *Afon Alaw*'s owner lived in Menai Bridge, and her crew—and their pets—are typical of seamen throughout the eighteenth and early nineteenth centuries

some of the most remarkable handiwork in a century notable for its craftsmen. Exquisite ship models in minute detail were carved from wood and ivory, every beam in place, each block, brace and buntline where it should be, and the gilt gingerbread work at the bow and stern reproduced with pinpoint accuracy. From whales' teeth and walrus tusks the whalers made cribbage boards, needle-cases, snuff-boxes and engraved busks for ladies' corsets. Even ordinary workaday items like sea-chests, lanyards and mats were decorated with intricate carving and complicated knot-work requiring hours of patient labour. Somehow these hard-bitten men found the inspiration in their dangerous, uncompromising lives to turn out works of art from the simple raw materials around them.

4 Ships, Men and Cargoes

At three in the afternoon the tide turned.

Half an hour before, the last chattering, waving group of visitors had been herded down the long gangway to stand in the grey drizzle of the quayside, staring up at the white faces of relatives clustered at the ship's rail. On the dockside longshoremen helped to single up the massive mooring lines at head and stern, casting the heavy coir eyes off their iron bollards while the crew hauled them aboard through the fairleads.

As the first pair of lines splashed into the murky water beside the quay, the captain's wife and two small sons appeared at the top of the gangway, escorted by the captain himself, still in shoregoing clothes of sober black with a gold watch-chain looped across his waistcoat. Gripping the ivory knob of her umbrella firmly in one hand and the small fingers of her younger son in the other, the captain's wife hurried down the gangway to the dockside where she turned to look up again at the tall ship making ready to sail.

Moments before the longshoremen hauled

(*Above*) the quayside of Waterloo Dock, Liverpool, in the 1860s

(*Left*) a small barque leaves a Liverpool dock in the mid-eighteenth century, watched by a motley crowd of seamen and sightseers

A brigantine enters Yarmouth harbour in rough weather, towed by the paddle-tug *United Service*. Strong tides can make this a difficult manoeuvre

the gangway ashore, the pilot pushed his way through the crowd of onlookers and went aboard to join the master on deck. Beyond the bow a cloud of acrid black fumes indicated that a tug had arrived to tow the ship out into the river, and seconds later its weighted heaving-line snaked on to the forecastle-head bringing with it a huge hawser to be slipped over the bitts in the bow. On the quay the remaining mooring lines were cast off, and with a quick blast of her whistle the little tug began to take the strain.

Ahead of the ship the water foamed and churned as the tug's paddles threshed with ponderous effort. Slowly the bowsprit and jib-boom began to point away from the wharf as the ship's head came round towards the river and began to move slowly in the wake of the tug. At the wheel the helmsman craned his neck to keep the tug's mast and the top of its grimy smokestack in view over the high bow, the only clue he would have to the tugmaster's intentions.

As the square-rigger pulled out into the

river a fair wind caught the ensign fluttering at the peak of her mizzen-gaff and the owner's house-flag streaming at the main truck; the mate barked an order and men began to swarm up the rigging to the topsail yards to cast off the gaskets which had held the sails neatly stowed in port. From the lofty yards they could watch the sturdy little tug puffing and clanking as it soldiered past the anchored shipping, and the grey skyline of the city already receding astern.

As the ship reached clearer water the top-sails began to belly out from the yards and were sheeted home on the deck below. Gradually the ship gathered way of her own and began to overhaul the valiantly thundering tug. When the long jib-boom loomed above her stern the tug quickly retrieved the towing hawser and sheered away with a pompous toot of her steam-whistle. Now lifting to the on-coming swell as canvas billowed on her fore-yard, the ship headed for the bar and open sea.

Scenes like these were an everyday sight in the river Mersey in the 1860s. Liverpool

The old Liverpool Customs House in 1861, overlooking the bustle of Salthouse Dock

Docks stretched from Canada Dock in the north to Brunswick in the south; across the river at Birkenhead new dock walls were going up round the Great Float and other basins were in the process of enlargement, giving an air of prosperity and enterprise to the whole area.

In the docks a forest of masts and spars towered more than a hundred feet into the air, dwarfing the warehouses and five-storey office buildings in nearby streets. As far as the eye could see along the waterfront the sky was criss-crossed by lofty topmasts and slatted yards while a maze of spidery rigging stretched to the decks below.

Out in the river big side-wheelers passed on their way to Canada Dock where the wide entrance could take their huge paddles; ocean-going steamers made for the sea on their way across the North Atlantic, passengers crowding the rail for a last sight of home. In and out between these vessels fishing-boats, coasting schooners and pilot cutters threaded their way, creating a constant pattern of movement on the grey Mersey.

Once they were securely berthed in dock the sailing ships took on a new character. The proud, graceful vessels which made their way into the river responsive to tide and wind became silent, echoing vaults beside the quay. Armies of stevedores tramped up and down their gangways, plundering the holds through gaping hatches. Grain, timber, tobacco, salt, textiles, fruit and cotton came and went while carpenters sawed and planed, replacing storm-damaged planking and splintered spars. Out-going vessels were loaded with drums of paint, kegs of nails, hanks of tarry marline, casks of lamp-oil and coils of thick manilla rope.

Downwind of Albert Dock drifted the exotic smell of spices as boxes and barrels were hoisted from the holds of returning East Indiamen and sent spinning five storeys into the air, to the top floor of a warehouse. Even on a sunny day this dock had a sombre look, $17\frac{1}{2}$ acres of water surrounded by high buildings, with one side perpetually in shadow behind its arched and colonnaded facade.

Nearby Salthouse Dock was a more cheer-

The trading ketch *Windward* joins other small craft in Liverpool's Salthouse Dock, with the Customs House in the background

ful place, and no less busy. The bowsprits and long jib-booms of several large sailing ships always projected over the quay as they lined up across the dock, their chain bobstays and martingales the target of small boys' acrobatics. Mountains of casks and kegs were stacked on the flagged wharf by chandlers' carts from the city; thin, scraggy dogs snuffed around these new arrivals until some harassed steward chased them off. There would be little enough in the casks to last a crew all the way to the Far East, and the steward would have his work cut out to find any surplus to supplement his wages.

It was simple fare at the best of times— boxes of hard biscuits, barrels of flour and meal, casks of dried peas and vinegar, salt pork and the ubiquitous 'salt horse', beef of dubious quality but great antiquity. For the first few days out of port there would be fresh vegetables too, the last anyone aboard would see for months.

Next door to Canning Dock was a graving basin where ships had weed and barnacles scraped from their copper sheathing, or the caulking renewed in their seams. Round this dock the smell of warm pitch mingled with the usual dockland odours of salt and horses as the old caulking was knocked out from between the planks of the hull, new oakum hammered in and the seams made watertight with sticky black tar. Nearby huge anchors

55

(*Below*) a sail-loft in the extensive upper-storey
of a dockside building

lay unshipped beside fathoms of chain and coils of manilla rope as thick as a man's wrist.

Down in the dry well of the dock stood the foreman shipwright, a bundle of plans under his arm as he pointed with a folded footrule at the next sprung plank to be tackled.

Solemn groups of shipowners strolled through the docks, gravely inspecting a new purchase or discussing current freight rates. In their tall silk hats and frock coats they looked affluent and influential, the autocrats reviewing their empire.

Standing nearby might be two or three sailing-ship masters, deep in conversation about vessels and passages. Chance meetings in port were often the only opportunity these men had to catch up with the news or talk over common problems and frustrations, since the position of command usually made the master the most isolated man on any ship. Bearded and dark-suited they looked far more sombre in their high silk hats than the steamer captains resplendent in gold-braided coats and gold-laced caps. One or two shipping-lines insisted, however, that their

sailing masters also wore uniform. (Leyland's of Liverpool were said to be the last firm to expect captains, on pain of instant dismissal, to turn up at their offices in gold braid.)

Not far from the Dock Board buildings were the sail-lofts where sailmakers and their apprentices spread bolts of tough 24-in canvas across the floor, cutting and sewing sails which would be tested by some of the worst weather in the world. These lofts occupied the upper storeys of dock buildings, the long open spaces under the eaves where no partitions or pillars could hamper the laying out of canvas. Behind the large windows the sailmakers sewed and cut on long benches with racks at one end to take the spikes for separating strands of rope, wooden fids, a sail-hook, a heaving-mallet for tightening up stitches and the tallow-filled horns which held their strong sail-needles.

The sailmaker's job was vitally important. On his skill depended the efficiency of a ship's motive power; if the sails didn't draw properly or spilled the wind from their edges, no vessel would make a fast passage. The

(*Below*) the crew of a sailing ship taking a sail
to be repaired

shape of each sail was determined by years of
experience and a good sailmaker would cut
the roach—the curve of the lower edge—by
eye alone, making up the finished sail from
seamed strips of canvas.

Along the after side of each edge a bolt-
rope was cross-stitched in position to prevent
splitting or stretching, the sailmaker pushing
his needle through rope and canvas with a
hard leather 'palm' tied across his hand. One
of the big mainsails could be 95ft wide and
weigh almost a ton, requiring the efforts of the
whole crew to take it up to its yard.

An ocean-going vessel would carry a suit
of heavy-weather sails, stronger and tougher
than the fair-weather set used in the tropics
and the Equatorial calms. Long rolls of spare
sails were kept in the ship's sail-locker,
labelled at one end with the mast and yard to
which they belonged. Most sizeable ships
carried a sailmaker of their own to patch and
repair sails during the voyage or even make
new ones when necessary.

If a sudden squall caught the ship un-
awares, a sail might carry away with a noise
like a pistol shot, ripping the heavy canvas
out of its bolt-ropes and shredding it to
ribbons in seconds. Cautious masters hounded
by penny-pinching shipowners would settle
for an unspectacular passage rather than
hazard their expensive sails by carrying too
much canvas in bad weather. Their unfortunate crews would find themselves sent
aloft time after time to take in sail or set it
again as every slight change in the wind had
its effect on the captain's confidence.

Traits like these would be discussed by
seamen of all nationalities in every corner of
the docks. Some strode along the wharves to a
new ship, sea-chest on shoulder, or sat
contentedly on the iron bollards smoking
yellowed clay pipes. There were wizened old
men with rope-scarred hands and faces
seamed by years of wild weather, tall fair
Scandinavians in sea-boots, whalers with
exotic tattoos and scrimshaw-handled knives,
and the hard-case 'packet-rats' who took on
the toughest ships and the toughest masters.

These men would have every ship in port
sized up by the time it was over the bar.

Dockland gossip would soon have its entire history, the whims and habits of its master, the last port of call and the kind of repair it was in, and from this the seamen made up their minds whether or not to sign on.

No one very much wanted to sail in the American ship *Dreadnought*, the 'Wild Boat of the Atlantic' which put in to Liverpool with grain for the last time in 1868. The long dark hull was instantly recognisable—this was a vessel in which both ship and men were driven hard. The owners accepted freights for delivery within a fixed time; one day too long at sea, and the cargo was carried free.

Inevitably this placed a tremendous burden on the men in command. *Dreadnought*'s most famous master was Captain Samuels, a good seaman but a man obsessed with cutting the passage time between Liverpool and New Jersey to the absolute minimum. This, he claimed, was just over nine days, and with his target set he drove his crew night and day to achieve it. It was said that he once spent a year in prison after shooting three men idling on the foreyard instead of getting on with their work.

As a result of this reputation Captain Samuels had to find a new crew where he could, a mixture of shanghaied landsmen picked up in port, and 'pierhead jumpers' who leaped aboard as the ship was hauled out through the dock gates. These men had no spare clothing or seagoing kit, and were often on the run from the police. They were joined

(*Above*) emigrant families waiting at the quayside for a passage to the New World

(*Left*) Prince's Dock, Liverpool, in the 1890s, as prosaic steam gradually spelled the end of the tall ships

in the forecastle by a stiffening of 'packet-rats', their faces scarred by knife-fights and their fingers marked by the use of deadly brass knuckles.

The packet-rats would go aloft in mid-winter wearing only a thin cotton shirt and tattered dungarees; it took the toughest mate to keep them in line, and even he had to be ready to enforce orders with his fists.

In this no-holds-barred world the 'bucko' mates developed a technique of 'hazing' their crews—working them remorselessly at un-necessary tasks in the hope that they would desert as soon as the ship berthed, leaving their wages unclaimed. When the penniless packet-rats joined another vessel they would soon re-equip themselves from the belongings of terrified shipmates.

For anyone who didn't belong amid the trundling carts, the shipwrights, the sail-makers and shore-going seamen, the docks could be a bewildering place. Huddled in miserable groups the emigrants felt uneasy and apprehensive; they were suddenly very much aware of leaving their homeland for whatever hardships were in store on the way to the promise of a better life.

How bad the voyage might be they could only imagine. By this time steamships had captured most of the transatlantic passenger trade, setting a new standard of comfort at sea, but, for many sailing-ship owners, emigrants were still a convenient outward cargo to Australia where wool or wheat could be loaded for the return trip. On these long voyages sailing ships could compete more successfully with steamers, especially when their sailing dates were linked to the Australian harvest.

Emigrants could still find a cheap passage to Australia in the 'tween-decks of the older sailing ships, the damp darkness immediately under the main deck. Their baggage was strictly limited and they were told to bring various cooking utensils, a jug for fresh water, cutlery and some basic food supplies. During the three-month voyage they lived mainly on salt beef and pork, tinned mutton, hard biscuits, highly smoked bacon and a few

badly preserved vegetables, eked out with rice or sago puddings which had to be made with salt water when the fresh supply ran out.

Once on board the emigrants had to make themselves as comfortable as they could, but even these conditions were a vast improvement on earlier ships. In the 1830s and '40s cheap emigrant quarters on ships sailing to America and Canada were nothing short of squalid, with tiers of wooden bunks crammed into the gloomy 'tween-decks, each one designed to hold four people at a time. If the emigrants couldn't afford a mattress, they had to lie on bare boards or negotiate with the unscrupulous waterfront traders for poor quality goods at high prices.

Below decks there was no privacy at all unless some kind of curtain could be rigged up round the bunk, and any disease ran wild in the dirty, cramped quarters. In bad weather the hatches leading to the deck above were closed and battened down. The emigrants were left to cook, sleep, wash or even relieve themselves as best they could, packed into the 'tween-decks by the light of a candle-lantern, thrown off their feet as the ship rolled and plunged, listening apprehensively to every crash of the sea or creak of timber.

In 1842 'Charles Dickens, Esquire, and Lady' travelled to America in the *Britannia* steam packet, and returned some time later in a sailing ship with a hundred disillusioned emigrants in the steerage accommodation. His account of these voyages appears in *American Notes*, an entertaining and sometimes moving description of conditions aboard these ships—life was often uncomfortable in the saloon but it was unspeakably hard for the poverty-stricken emigrants returning with shattered dreams from the Land of Promise.

Dickens' dismay on first inspecting the

(*Above*) in the older emigrant ships this confined space below decks served for eating, sleeping and recreation

(*Above right*) *Charlotte Rhodes* and *Freebooter* tied up at the Old Quay, Exeter

(*Below right*) seen from the mizzen shrouds, *Charlotte Rhodes* heads across the North Sea on her way to Rotterdam

(*Overleaf*) the iron steam-ship *Great Britain*, which set a new standard of comfort on the passage to Australia. Unfortunately, even the *Great Britain* was subject to bad weather at sea

saloon aboard the steam-packet—'not unlike a gigantic hearse with windows in the sides'—was equalled only by his horror at the lack of space and sparse furnishings in his state-room below decks. His upper berth comprised 'a very flat quilt, covering a very thin mattress, spread like a surgical plaster on a most inaccessible shelf'; the seating accommodation was confined to two hard horsehair benches against one side of the cabin, and the tiny room was lit by a small porthole and a single lamp after dark. The quality of life was not improved by the livestock carried on board for the comfort of saloon passengers, which made its presence unpleasantly obvious.

But however spartan these quarters, they were a hundred times better than the conditions endured by the emigrants on the sailing ship. 'Some of them,' relates Dickens, 'had been in America but three days, some but three months, and some had gone out in the last voyage of that very ship in which they were returning home. Others had sold their clothes to raise the passage-money, and had hardly rags to cover them; others had no food, and lived on the charity of the rest; and one man, it was discovered nearly at the end of the voyage . . . had had no substance whatever but the bones and scraps of fat he took from plates used in the after-cabin dinner, when they were put out to be washed.'

These people had been loaded aboard by an unscrupulous company which had chartered the entire 'tween-deck space of the ship, packing as many wretched creatures into it as they could for the outward passage, lured by tales of the riches to be had in America. Without proper food or medical attention they endured the dreadful journey across the Atlantic, only to discover when they got there that even if they could find work they would be no better paid than they had been at home. Back they came, poorer than ever, having sold everything they possessed to pay for their passage out.

By the 1860s conditions had improved with the division of emigrant sleeping accommodation into cabins and dormitories and the establishment of proper recreation space.

The huge steamer *Great Britain* was for 15 years an auxiliary sailing ship on the Australian run. If the wind was steady and favourable, sails were set; in calms or bad weather she could still continue on her course with smoke puffing from her twin funnels and steam turning her massive 15ft propeller. In her 322ft hull she carried 730 passengers in relative—if graded—comfort.

'This celebrated Auxiliary Steam Clipper,' boomed the sailing-bill, 'fitted with oscillating engines: Steam from Liverpool to Australia in 60 Days.'

It went on, 'Her Saloon arrangements are perfect, and combine every possible convenience—Ladies' Boudoir, Baths, etc.—and her noble passenger decks, lighted at intervals by sideports, offer unrivalled accommodation for all classes.'

First-class passengers could expect a high standard of cuisine and a fully equipped cabin for 75 guineas; at 30 guineas second-class passengers were responsible for their own bedding, soap and linen, and were expected to pay for any damage they might do to the cabin fittings. Third-class and steerage passengers paid between 14 and 20 guineas, and were expected to bring cutlery, cups and plates, and a pot to hold fresh water. To make their basic fare more palatable they could bring a certain amount of bacon, ham and pickles, or buy them on board from the purser.

Even on the *Great Britain* no-one could guarantee a dry trip. In the rolling seas of the south Atlantic the *Great Britain*'s passenger accommodation could be a wet place where bedding became damp and rivulets of water sloshed to and fro across the deck. To their dismay lady passengers found their shoes and the hems of their long dresses sodden with seawater; in spite of boudoirs and noble passenger decks sea-sickness could still make it a miserable voyage.

(*Above left*) 'Captain Mac', complete with cigar, at the wheel of *Charlotte Rhodes*

On a cold, blustery day, a film crew watches *Marquès* at anchor

The *Great Britain*'s best-known master, Captain John Gray, would have fitted admirably on the bridge of any modern cruise liner. Rumour said he was the runaway son of a peer, which caused many female hearts to flutter; whatever his background, he spent much of his time talking to his passengers, patting their children on the head and explaining the ship's manoeuvres to them with a patience rare among his colleagues.

(Left) aboard Brunel's *Great Eastern*. Above the broad decks, funnels sprout between the masts

With ornamental oil-lamps and a fountain, the first-class accommodation at sea could be very luxurious

On some passenger ships there was more to put up with than discomfort. Rats were attracted to the stores of food, but didn't confine themselves to the lower decks. At night they pattered about behind the panelling of the cabins, occasionally scuttling across the floor if they found a way in. Perhaps the hazards of the journey bred a new, resourceful strain of Victorian lady, for, instead of fainting helplessly away, even female passengers set about attacking the rats with a shoe or whatever was nearest to hand.

Accommodation at sea improved rapidly. In 1872 the White Star Line introduced gas lighting in the *Adriatic*, operated from a gas plant next to the engine room. By 1883 the Belfast Steamship Company's *Dynamic* was lit throughout by electricity.

By the 1870s, too, water no longer had to be fetched in jugs and jars. Purpose-built fittings had begun to appear in cabins—a washbowl recessed into the top of a locker, with a proper plug which could be removed to allow the water to drain into the sea. Fresh water was now piped to the cabins—cold, but at least running from a tap.

Instead of a wooden shelter on deck with a lavatory leading somewhere over the ship's side and chamber-pots in the staterooms, there were now better facilities adjoining the cabins and sometimes even a bathroom where a hot bath could be had.

In the early 1890s the Cunard Line launched the *Campania* and the *Lucania*, the last word in floating elegance. Twice as long as the *Great Britain*, they were twin-screw steamers with accommodation for 600 first-class, 400 second-class and over 700 third-class passengers. To run the ship took a crew of 244, with 180 more to look after the passengers; the first-class dining saloon alone was 100ft long and 62ft wide, seating over 400 people in revolving armchairs, with 'nooks and corners' round the sides for anyone who wanted to dine in curtained seclusion.

Satinwood, mahogany, cedar, pine, ivory, gilding and brocade were used in profusion with Persian carpets and tiles; gilt tritons and nymphs soared above a grand piano and an American organ. There was a 'Scottish-baronial-style smoking-room and a 1,000-volume library, single and double berthed cabins and 'family rooms'. For those to whom expense was no object there were suites of rooms in mahogany and satinwood with a 'boudoir' complete with chairs and mirrors, a private lavatory and a bedroom with a brass bedstead and a wardrobe.

The second-class passengers, on the other hand, had to make do with an American walnut smoking-room and a cottage piano, although they could console themselves with a quart of champagne for seven shillings, a sixpenny cigar or a four-shilling bottle of whisky—one way to alleviate the rigours of travel.

5 A Real-life James Onedin

One day in 1851, so the story goes, a small, energetic, red-haired man called James Baines was walking along the cobbled wharf of Queen's Dock in Liverpool when he noticed a very elderly ship with a broom tied to one stumpy masthead. This was the usual signal that a vessel was for sale, so Baines went over for a closer look.

The ship was certainly no beauty; grimy and neglected, she lay beside the dock wall, her rigging frayed and slack, and paint peeling in rotted ribbons from her bulwarks. Built many years before on Canada's Miramichi River, the ship had been given short, squat masts and bows so bluff that speed was obviously out of the question.

Several Liverpool shipowners had already looked her over, sneered, and dubbed her 'the pork barrel'. This didn't bother James Baines, who strongly suspected that in the 1850s any vessel which would carry emigrants to the shores of the New World could make her owner's fortune. To the immense amusement of the local shipowners he decided to buy the old ship.

Rumours had reached Britain of a huge gold strike in Australia and already the rush was beginning, just as it had when gold was found in California. Would-be miners were arriving in Liverpool by the score, clamouring for a passage to the gold-fields. In Australia whole towns had emptied as gold-hunters swarmed into the outback, leaving their homes and their jobs for the lure of possible riches. Shopkeepers found themselves without assistants, fine houses were cleared of servants—it was even said that the Governor of Victoria

James Baines, whose shipping empire included some of the most famous sailing vessels of all time

now groomed his horse with his own hands.

Bearded miners back from the diggings swaggered through the Melbourne streets bent on spending their money as fast as they made it, and then going back for more. One man who went to Australia to open a circus returned home after less than a year with a profit of £30,000.

'Champagne for all' was the order of the day, and tall tales of nuggets strewn around like pebbles on a river-bed inflamed the general frenzy. Ships arriving at Sydney, Melbourne and Adelaide were soon deserted by their crews, and lay idle in the harbours with no means of starting for home.

To the first wave of fortune-seekers from Britain the hardships of a long passage to Australia were irrelevant as long as they reached the diggings before all the gold ran out. They wanted a ship—any kind of ship—and James Baines was happy to oblige them.

In 1852 alone 36,250 emigrants left Liverpool for Australia; by 1857 the total had reached 155,600.

This story of Baines' first venture as a shipowner may well be apocryphal, but the man himself was unlikely to deny it. In the days of flying clippers and their astonishingly fast passages, when a shipmaster might even suggest setting his wife's petticoat as an extra sail, James Baines well knew the value of a dashing reputation. A small man—only five feet three or four inches in height—he was never seen without a frock coat, high collar and bow tie. What he lacked in stature he made up in energy, and he was well known at the Exchange or in the docks for his constant animation and chatter. As he began to make his name in shipping circles he also became known as a 'soft touch', always susceptible to a good hard-luck story.

Baines was born in 1823 in Upper Duke Street, Liverpool, where his mother kept a confectioner's shop. She must have been a baker of considerable talent: she was once called upon to make a cake for the wedding of Queen Victoria, and for many years after her death Liverpool seamen who had been regular customers as boys fondly remembered her handmade cakes.

As a young man Baines took up an engineering apprenticeship, but soon abandoned it because, as he admitted later, he hated dirty work and having to get up early in the morning. Fortunately his uncle was a Liverpool shipbroker, and the fastidious James went to work for the family firm. Either through his inspired purchase of the 'pork-barrel', or by a more gradual process of partnerships and investment, Baines soon became a shipowner himself and acquired a reputation for shrewdness and foresight.

These qualities stood him in good stead in

1852, when a Canadian-built three-decker made her maiden voyage from Mobile to Liverpool with a cargo of cotton. In Liverpool she was bought at a bargain price by Paddy McGee, a well known and rather shady character who kept a marine store in the city. From McGee the ship swiftly changed hands again, this time to James Baines who had noticed that in spite of her ample beam the hollow bows at her waterline were built for speed.

Launched at Smith's yard in New Brunswick, the *Marco Polo* had massive 'port-painted' sides (traditionally supposed to make the pirates of the China Sea believe a ship carried guns), eight feet of headroom between decks and sturdy masts and spars designed to

The fastidious James Baines as a young man

VANDYKE & BROWN
PHOTOGRAPHERS

OLD ST & 34 CASTLE ST
LIVERPOOL

carry a great spread of sail in gale-force winds.

Baines refitted his new ship for the top-class emigrant trade, sparing no expense. A special cabin was provided under the poop for the exclusive use of lady passengers, and forward of this an impressive saloon. This apartment was the showpiece of the vessel; the ceiling was panelled in maple, the supporting pilasters decorated with pieces of mirror and foreign coins, and the upholstery covered in velvet and brocade.

As an ultimate luxury the doors of the saloon were embellished with the twin allegorical figures of Commerce and Industry in glowing stained glass—Baines knew where his best interests lay. In the centre of the floor a large table made of thick plate-glass served as a skylight for the sleeping accommodation below.

With all this magnificence to offer, Baines pulled no punches in his advertising: 'It is the largest vessel ever dispatched from Liverpool to Australia,' trumpeted the sailing-bill, 'and is expected to sail as fast as any ship afloat.'

Thanks to Baines' keen eye for a potentially fast ship and the seamanship of her master, James Nicol Forbes, *Marco Polo* was destined to become one of the most famous ships in an age of record-breakers. Her first passage to Melbourne and back took the unbelievable time of five months and twenty-one days; the story is told that Baines, informed by one of the dock-workers that his ship had returned to the Mersey, refused to believe it was true until he had seen her with his own eyes.

Captain Forbes, whose modesty was not a strong point, brought his ship into the river sporting a canvas banner slung between her masts which read 'The Fastest Ship in the World'. In her cabin *Marco Polo* carried gold dust worth £100,000 and a 340oz nugget, a gift from the colony of Victoria to the Queen.

By 1858 James Baines' Black Ball Line owned 86 ships and employed 3,000 seamen and some 300 officers. The business was so solidly established that even the failure of Liverpool Borough Bank, with debts of more than £4,000,000, turned out to be only a temporary setback.

In the mid 1850s Baines' shrewd assessment of coming trends led him to order four remarkable vessels from the American shipbuilding genius Donald McKay. *Lightning*, *Champion of the Seas*, *James Baines* and *Donald McKay* were among the most famous ships ever to be launched from his yard in Boston; each vessel was designed separately, but all four were built for great speed in strong winds.

Lightning was the first and fastest of the quartet. Not counting her stunsails on their long booms, some thirty separate sails drove her hollow bows through the waves, and she possessed the ultimate in seagoing panache, a moonsail set above the skysail on her mainmast, 160ft above the deck. In those days if an extra piece of canvas could add half a knot to a ship's speed, it would be set.

To add to this magnificence the semi-elliptical stern was embellished with gilt carving and at her bow the full-length figure of a woman with flowing hair and swirling white robes held a golden thunderbolt defiantly towards the sea.

With the redoubtable Bully Forbes as master, *Lightning* set off for Melbourne; the return passage took 63 days and made shipping history.

Several years later *Lightning* was said to have scored another less popular 'first'. One hot December evening in 1859 the clipper landed a consignment of animals and birds at Geelong in Australia. The assorted British wildlife was on its way to Mr Thomas Austin, a keen sportsman who missed his favourite diversion on the other side of the world and had decided to import some game to shoot. Among the animals which made the long trip from the English countryside were twenty-six wild rabbits which promptly set to work to produce the millions which plague Australia today.

Apart from their distinctive red-and-black house flag Baines' Black Ball ships could easily be identified by their combination of black hull, white masts, black yards and black mastheads. The passenger ships carried surgeons, chaplains, and sometimes even a brass band, while stowed in the saloon were boards for chess, backgammon and draughts for the passengers' diversion; in good weather there was dancing on the poop after dinner and concerts featuring popular sentimental melodies like *A Life on the Ocean Wave* and *The Death of Nelson*. Under a good captain the food was generally of a high standard, and for first-class passengers verged on the sumptuous; five courses were usual at dinner, with an impressive variety of roast and cold meat, pasta, fish of all kinds and elaborate puddings and confectionery.

These halcyon days lasted until the late 1860s. Baines eventually moved to a luxurious house in Princes Park where he kept a large staff of servants including five maids, a coachman and a groom. With typical generosity he made arrangements for them all to visit the theatre once a week, in relays, while he and his wife went driving round Liverpool in their coach-and-four, showering family and friends with gifts. At the same time a combination of financial depression and civil war in America brought many ships onto the market quite cheaply, and Baines the shipping magnate thought nothing of buying five vessels in one morning at Kellock's auction rooms.

As the maritime world turned more and more to steam, Baines experimented with steamers himself. As early as 1855 his ship *Vestal* left for Balaclava with a cargo of mail for the military hospitals at Malta and Scutari, and in the 1860s the ss *Pennsylvania* made regular passages between Liverpool and New York. On the longer haul to Australia a steamer was at no great advantage and could be eclipsed by a sailing ship with favourable winds. Perhaps the impulsive Baines found the world of steamers too prosaic after the romance of sail; somehow this side of his business never really prospered.

By this time the big softwood clippers, so fast when they first left McKay's Boston yard, were becoming strained and waterlogged. The American ships which Baines had bought at bargain prices were also getting past their prime. Their passages took longer, and repair bills mounted. The mad rush to Australia had dwindled to a trickle, and emigrants had started to farm and raise sheep with a resulting change in the trade with Britain. Ships were now returning with cargoes of hides,

(*Right*) Captain Baines comes aboard the *Charlotte Rhodes*

(*Below*) Sydney harbour, Australia, with both sail and steam in evidence

wool and tallow, and Baines' big vessels with their generous headroom below decks were not so suitable for this work as the smaller teak and composite ships coming from yards in Aberdeen, Liverpool and on Clydeside.

At 2 am on Sunday 31 October 1869, the magnificent *Lightning* had almost finished loading wool at Yarra Street pier in Geelong when someone noticed smoke spiralling from her hull. It was soon obvious that the fire had a good hold and the ship was doomed; fire was a constant risk with a wool cargo, which could burst into flames quite spontaneously if the bales became damp when they were stowed in the waiting vessel.

To protect other shipping in the harbour *Lightning*'s master ordered the blazing clipper to be cast off from the dock and she drifted slowly out into Corio Bay. Working against time, stevedores unloaded some of her cargo of wool into lighters while carpenters made holes in her planking at the waterline in an attempt to scuttle the ship before she could damage any others. In the intense heat *Lightning*'s iron foremast melted and fell overboard; reluctant to sink, she burned all day while guns were fired erratically from the wharf to enlarge the holes made by the carpenters.

Finally at sundown the *Lightning* sank in 24ft of water 200yd offshore, leaving only the charred stumps of her masts visible above the surface.

Her days as a crowd-puller were not quite at an end even then. A few months later, anxious to be rid of the dangerous wreck, the authorities accepted an offer of £1,995 to have what was left of the ship blown up with explosives. Divers loaded sixteen charges of 150lb each into the hull, and on Thursday 21 April sightseers thronged the wharf to watch the Mayor of Geelong detonate the explosion.

To everyone's disappointment *Lightning*'s strong timbers defied the blast, and the expected bang only produced a dull thump beneath the waters of the bay. It was enough, though, to loosen the fastenings of the clipper's hull, and gradually over the next few months the famous ship finally broke up.

Baines' business had already suffered a severe blow when Barned's Bank collapsed carrying several large companies with it, and he admitted later that this marked the start of a slow disintegration of the Black Ball Line.

In 1872 his wife died, and Baines moved house twice in the next two years, finally giving up his home altogether when his two elder daughters were married. In 1882 he sold his last ship, the *Seraphina*, and went back to the business he had started in—shipbroking. By this time his business flair had almost deserted him, and he was cheated by unscrupulous partners of his share in the sale of a ship called the *Three Brothers*. Baines took the case to court, but never recovered his money.

This failure undermined his health and—more importantly—his morale. The former energy and enthusiasm were dissipated, the flair and foresight gone. He died at sixty-six of cirrhosis of the liver, nursed by Mrs Isbister, the wife of a dock worker in whose house he had been lodging.

'No one is more eager to make money than me,' he once said, 'but when I do, it goes very quickly.' Although his fortune may have gone, James Baines' reputation lives on wherever the flying clippers are remembered, as a man who had the good fortune—and the good sense—to own some of the most famous sailing ships ever built.

(*Above left*) Anne Stallybrass as James Onedin's faithful and resourceful wife, Anne, who died giving him the child he wanted

(*Left*) Brian Rawlinson as Robert Onedin and Howard Lang as the crusty Captain Baines

6 James Nicol Forbes:
'Hell or Melbourne in 60 Days'

In the great days of sail every seaman could tell tales of hard-living, two-fisted captains beating their terrified crews back from the royal halliards with a belaying-pin or quelling mutinies with a six-shooter and the galley cleaver. In most cases these were empty legends, embroidered and exaggerated as they changed hands in ports all over the world. Occasionally, though, there might be a basis in fact, and the reality behind many of the legends was Captain James Nicol Forbes. Although his reputation for fast passages in ships of the Black Ball Line vanished almost as swiftly as it came, he was undoubtedly one of the finest seamen of his day.

Born in Aberdeen in 1821, Forbes was the son of a prominent advocate. At an early age he was drawn to the sea and ships, and his father wisely allowed him to learn the rudiments of navigation at a little school in Marischal Street. From there his seafaring career took him to Glasgow and eventually to Liverpool, where he arrived penniless at the age of eighteen and started to work his way up through the ranks to a command.

Forbes first came to the notice of James Baines in 1849 when he was given command of the new ship *Wilson Kennedy*, built in Quebec for Martin Brothers of Liverpool. Forbes went to Canada to take charge of the vessel and bring it across the Atlantic to its new owners. Anxious to make a name for himself, he pressed the new ship to its limit and turned the maiden voyage into a respectably fast passage, fast enough to attract the attention of the Liverpool shipowners.

After joining the Black Ball Line Forbes first commanded the small barque *Cleopatra* before moving to the larger *Maria*. Neither of these vessels had outstanding sailing qualities, but Forbes forced them to make good passages by crowding on sail until the last possible moment.

Both Baines and Forbes shared a talent for publicity and showmanship, although they were quite unalike in temperament. Forbes was mercurial, a man of instant decisions, ruthless and apparently quite without fear.

In one command, while his ship heeled dramatically before a gale, Forbes would work his way out along the swinging boom of a lower stunsail, far beyond the bulwarks; there he would perch, surveying his vessel as she ploughed through the waves. It would have taken very little—a sudden squall or a shift of the wind—to carry away both the spar and the man clinging to it, but the possibility didn't seem to occur to Forbes. Perhaps he just enjoyed tempting Providence.

A captain who drove a fine ship to its limit was inevitably a gambler; to carry full sail while the wind rose to gale force meant risking sails and spars at the very least; at worst it meant a possible dismasting under the terrific strain and maybe even the loss of a ship. If the master's luck held he could make a fast passage and his own reputation, but if his judgement was less than sound, lives could be lost.

Portrait of a tall ship. The port-painted *Macquarie*, one of the best-known vessels in the Australian trade

Passengers aboard *Macquarie* promenade or lie in
the sun on the poop. Deck games or a brisk walk
round the ship was their only exercise during
nearly four months at sea

A sailing-bill for the steam-clipper *Royal Charter*

For many years it seemed as if Forbes
possessed the two qualities vital for the
achievement of record passages, gambler's
luck and the intuition of a fine seaman.

After his two minor commands under the
Black Ball flag Forbes was appointed master
of the newly refitted *Marco Polo*. At a lavish
dinner on board on the eve of her departure
for Australia he announced with confidence
that he hoped to be back in the Mersey in a
little more than six months. As it turned out,
he improved on that estimate by nine days.

On his second voyage as master of the
Marco Polo, Forbes wrote to his employer
from mid-Atlantic:

We have boarded several vessels from
London with passengers, but my passengers say they would rather be on

board *Marco Polo* than any of them . . . We have had one death, a child seven months old, and one birth, which makes our number good. I have got about 40 of the expertest thieves on board from London, and, which is worse, two or three of them are in the first cabin. I will only add that I have not had one word of complaint against ship, provisions, master or officers, which is a great thing to say, and they are all going to write home to their friends to come out in your new ship.

This last claim was probably for Baines' benefit, since passengers had often been known to complain about the way Forbes drove his ships. Gilt pilasters and brocade cushions were little comfort when a vessel pitched in pounding seas under a great spread of canvas; crystal decanters flew from their racks, cutlery slid across the tables, soup splashed from its tureen and the passengers lurched and bumped their way round the ship.

The crew were often as terrified as the passengers, since they were in a better position to understand the risks their captain was taking. All the classic tales are told of 'Bully' Forbes—how he stood at the break of the poop urging on his cowering crew with a loaded revolver in each hand, or padlocked the running rigging to forestall any un-authorised attempt to shorten sail.

On one occasion an ashen passenger ventured on deck to find the ship groaning and creaking with the strain, and several sails on the point of carrying away. Desperately he begged the captain to reduce sail, only to hear Forbes growl that he intended to reach 'Hell or Melbourne' in 60 days flat.

However it was achieved, Forbes made another good passage in the *Marco Polo*, and Baines sent him to Boston to supervise the fitting-out of the *Lightning*. Forbes brought the big clipper back to Liverpool in 13 days 19½ hours and then went on to drive her out to Melbourne and back in a total of 140 days—77 days out and 63 back.

After this triumph Forbes was moved again, this time to the new Aberdeen-built emigrant ship *Schomberg*, prudently named after the government emigration agent in Liverpool. The vessel left the Mersey in a blaze of publicity in October 1855, but it was soon obvious that the *Schomberg* wasn't going to provide Forbes with another record passage. In spite of the signal '60 Days to Melbourne' flying from her halliards, lack of a steady wind delayed the crossing of the line until twenty-eight days after sailing; a series of frustrating calms held the ship back still further, until at half past ten in the evening on Boxing Day she ran aground on a sandspit off Curdies Inlet, 40 miles west of Cape Otway, the southernmost tip of Victoria. Luckily the ss *Queen*, on her way from Warrnambool, picked up the passengers and landed them at Melbourne.

At the subsequent enquiry Forbes and his officers were exonerated, but several grave doubts were cast over the conduct of the notorious captain. Lawyers hinted that he had lost interest in his sluggish ship and that when the first mate came to find him in the saloon to warn him that the ship was danger-ously near Cape Otway, Forbes snarled in disgust, 'Call me again when she's on the beach'. It was also suggested that when the ship tried to tack away from the dangerous sandspit Forbes had left it too late to manoeuvre, but couldn't drop anchor to save the vessel since the anchors were still stowed on deck just as they had been in mid-ocean.

Opinion among the passengers was divided. Most of the occupants of the saloon supported Forbes, claiming that he hardly left the deck within the sight of land. In contrast, the *Melbourne Age* published a report which alleged that 'the conduct of the captain, surgeon and officers of the *Schomberg* was ungentlemanly, discourteous and immoral'. The food, it went on, had been unfit to eat, and the surgeon had even retired to bed with one of his female patients.

Despite Forbes' efforts to clear his name in the British press the suspicion remained that he had purposely failed to save a ship whose sailing qualities disappointed him.

This disaster was followed by another tragedy, the death of Forbes' young wife, Jane. After this double blow nothing seemed to go well, and Forbes spent a spell 'on the beach' where the once ebullient captain was described by an acquaintance as 'a very sad and silent man'. Eventually James Baines gave him another chance—command of the *Hastings* in 1857—but Forbes' luck had at last run out, and the *Hastings* was lost off the Cape of Good Hope just before Christmas two years later.

Even at this point Forbes had not yet lost his self-respect. On the Hong Kong waterfront a few years later he was accosted by two American sailors who began to insult him; instantly Forbes tore off his coat and gave them a sound beating, leaving them in no doubt that the broken, down-at-heel seaman was still a man to be reckoned with.

Bully Forbes later made a brief comeback in the *General Wyndham*, carrying cotton from Charleston to the Mersey, and in 1867 Baines gave him back his old ship *Marco Polo*, then well past her prime. Three years after Baines finally sold her, Forbes died, a broken man at the age of fifty-two. His grave in a Liverpool cemetery is near the tomb of his former employer, and bears the simple inscription 'Master of the famous *Marco Polo*'.

Like many of the men who sailed them the magnificent ships too became old and unwanted before their time or suffered a sad end by wreck or by fire.

In April 1858 the *James Baines* was unloading her cargo of jute, rice, linseed oil and hides from Calcutta in Huskisson Dock, Liverpool, when the tell-tale smell of burning fibres spread through the ship. The main hold was opened but the smoke was already too dense to see where the fire had started, and in spite of the desperate efforts of firemen and dockers flames began to engulf the ship.

There was nothing for it but to scuttle the vessel where she lay in the hope that seawater rushing into the hull would put out the flames. Unfortunately this was attempted just as the tide was starting to ebb, and the burn-ing ship settled gently on to the silt at the bottom of the basin where the fire raced the length of her hull, bringing down two masts on top of nearby warehouses.

Hastily the dock was cleared of other shipping, and the *James Baines* became a complete inferno with flames sucked skywards between the skins of her hull reflecting in a red glow over the docks. By the time the fire had burned itself out the once lovely clipper was reduced to a blackened hulk.

As the old softwood ships were gradually ousted from the Australian passenger trade by their iron counterparts, they found new cargoes in other places. Many of them ended up plying from the Chincha Islands with a hold full of unsavoury guano—a bird-dropping fertiliser much in demand in Europe—before slipping into the ship-killing timber trade between the St Lawrence River and Liverpool, less than twenty years after they were launched. *Red Jacket* and *Donald McKay* survived this treatment only to become coal-hulks in Madeira and the Cape Verde Islands. The *Three Brothers*, the ship that caused James Baines so much grief, ended her days as a coal hulk in Gibraltar.

The famous *Marco Polo* carried timber from Quebec across the Atlantic for many years, her stout frames standing up well to the wear and tear. Eventually in August 1883 she was wrecked on Prince Edward Island at the mouth of the St Lawrence, and a few days later her cargo and the remains of her hull were sold for a mere £600.

In Australian waters: the *Wave of Life* waits for a cargo at Sydney, New South Wales

Sailing ships loading timber on Canada's Mirachimi River in the last years of the nineteenth century

Loading timber through square bow-ports in the
St Lawrence River, Canada

7 Before the Mast

The great lexicographer Dr Samuel Johnson could never understand why any man should want to go to sea, let alone take a pride in his profession. 'I cannot account for that,' he said in 1759, 'any more than I can account for other strange perversions of the imagination . . . Being in a ship is being in a jail, with the chance of being drowned. A man in jail has more room, more food and commonly better company.'

For the ordinary seaman of the later nineteenth century, life on a sailing ship was always hard and often downright unpleasant. But while it astonished Dr Johnson that any-one should go to sea at all, it has to be remembered that life ashore for these men could be just as unpleasant.

Most merchant seamen first went to sea as boys of thirteen or fourteen, the earliest they could take part in the work of the ship. Few concessions were made to their youth; the weakest left the sea after one voyage or died of disease; the rest developed lean, muscular toughness on a combination of poor food and hard physical work.

Many boys were bound apprentice to a shipowner for four years. Gradually these apprentices came to be regarded as future officers, although the amount of instruction they received depended very much on the benevolence of the master, and whether he used them simply as cheap labour. One of the apprentices' tasks was to row their captain from ship to ship or ship to shore when the vessel was at anchor instead of alongside a quay, and a despotic master sometimes kept his boat's crew waiting in the chilly harbour until the small hours of next day while he sampled the attractions available ashore.

Going to sea at least represented the opportunity of earning a wage, however small. In the coastal communities and small ports round Britain the seafaring tradition was part of life from a boy's earliest years, and he automatically became a seaman as soon as he was old enough.

A new man joining a ship in the 1860s would report first to one of the mates, and

Aboard the *Torrens*, near the end of the nineteenth century: author Joseph Conrad with five apprentices who sailed in his ship

then be allotted a berth in the forecastle. From the early days of sail the seamen's traditional accommodation was in the old-style forecastle, below decks in the bow of the ship, often reached only by a small scuttle on the deck above which was also the source of light and ventilation. These quarters were frequently awash with seawater; in the worst weather the scuttle would be closed, condemning the men below to the stifling dark. The only furniture these forecastles contained was a line of hammocks slung from deck beams and the solid wooden sea-chests of the crew.

Although hammocks were still used in small merchant vessels until the turn of the century, fitted bunks gradually replaced them in larger ships—square coffin-like boxes with a gap in the side to crawl through. These bunks were not always watertight, and many older seamen preferred to sleep in a hammock with an oilskin rigged above it to keep out water dripping down from the deck seams.

In the coasting schooners master and crew ate together, but in larger ocean-going ships tables and benches were usually provided in the forecastle where the men could light a small stove to keep themselves warm and dry their clothes. In badly run ships the crew often had to steal coal for this stove from the galley, or from the cargo if it happened to be coal, and sometimes they even had to use fat from their food and strips of rag to make lamps to light their quarters.

Except for the 'idlers'—carpenter, bosun, cook and sailmaker, if one was carried—every member of the crew was allotted to a watch. The watches were picked by the mates who mustered all hands on deck soon after sailing and divided up the men between them. Each watch was then given its own side of the forecastle, port and starboard, so that the clump of feet and the murmur of voices wouldn't disturb those whose turn it was to snatch a few hours' sleep.

This arrangement was still used when crews were moved out of the cramped conditions of the old topgallant forecastle, which they had shared with the windlass and its cable, to a roomier deck-house abaft the foremast.

Where bunks were provided the seaman was expected to bring his own straw mattress —the 'donkey's breakfast'. All too often this became hopelessly sodden or the lodging-place of fleas and bed-bugs, with disastrous results. A crew was also expected to possess oilskins (cotton dipped in linseed oil mixed with boot-polish), knives, cutlery, plates, a tin mug, leather seaboots and enough clothes to keep them warm in cold weather, but this was by no means always the case. If a man had deserted from his previous ship he would often have left most of his belongings behind; those who arrived at the last minute by 'pierhead jump' were usually on the run from the forces of law and order, and were no better equipped. Even the men who signed on quite legally in port might well have lost their possessions in a crooked card-game or been robbed of what little they had in a cheap lodging-house.

One of the captain's privileges was a store known as the 'slop chest' from which he could issue tobacco, soap, clothing and other useful items at his own price, setting the cost against the wages of each member of the crew. As these tended to be little enough in any case—three or four pounds a month—a seaman could end up with next to nothing at the end of a voyage once fines had been paid for unruly behaviour or for losing equipment overboard.

Over the years, changes in maritime law improved the standard of provisions on merchant ships, but it was a long, slow process. As early as 1844 the rations for each member of the crew had to be set out in the Articles of Agreement they signed on joining a ship, but the number who could read or even arrived sober enough to do so was comparatively small. It wasn't until 1892 that a proper Inspectorate of Ships' Provisions was set up, and even then the inspectors had no power to examine the food before it left the supplier's premises.

Once the meagre supplies were stowed aboard, rats, cockroaches and maggots attacked the stores. For some reason cockroaches regarded ink as a delicacy and made life difficult for the steward by devouring the paper labels attached to the food.

In the days before refrigeration any provisions taken on a long voyage had to be preserved in some way. Traditionally British seamen had existed from ages past on salt beef and pork and hard biscuit—lumps of baked dough used at sea by the ancient Greeks and later by the Romans (many more recent British crews suspected they had been issued with the original article). The dough was beaten flat or put into moulds and baked as many as three times, occasionally being broken down into meal again after this and rebaked. Needless to say it became as hard as iron, and had to be softened with water before anyone could eat it.

If water spoiled the store of biscuits they were cooked again in the galley stove and any insects which had found their way in were baked inside them. The results must have been very grim. Former apprentices could often recall spare moments spent racing biscuit-weevils across a wooden table-top.

The salt beef and pork, too, tended to be pretty unpalatable. The beef was as hard as leather and the pork sometimes almost black, streaked with lines of green. Horse-meat was frequently substituted without anyone noticing the difference. In theory, properly salted meat should keep for thirty or forty years provided it was in good condition when the preserving was done, but casks were often damaged during loading operations or subjected to temperatures of 80 or 90 degrees in tropical latitudes; after this treatment they gave off a stomach-turning stench when they were eventually opened.

In the galley it was the cook's task to make this unpleasant stuff palatable. After prolonged soaking to remove the salt the meat was usually boiled and served with dumplings or dried peas, or mixed with ship's biscuit to form a kind of hash. Weekly rations included flour, tea, sugar and rice, most of which was issued to the galley for cooking purposes, together with the bulk of the fresh water ration.

Not all ships kept their crews hungry, although many seamen found provisions more generous on American vessels. Some British ships relieved the monotonous diet by adding marmalade, dried fruit and raisins to the list of supplies for the forecastle, with fresh meat and vegetables when the ship was in port.

As early as 1844 an Act of Parliament laid down the exact amount of antiscorbutic limejuice, sugar and vinegar to be issued to each man in a foreign-going vessel which had existed for ten days on salt meat. Without the lime-juice there was always a chance of scurvy; after a few weeks a man became weak and easily exhausted, and the least exertion could make him dizzy; his arms and legs began to swell and his gums started to bleed. In cold climates these symptoms set in even more rapidly, and men suddenly dropped dead while climbing out of their bunks. To guard against this, the lime-juice rule also applied to passengers in the cheap emigrant accommodation, who lived on more or less the same food as the crew.

On bigger British ships there was a considerable contrast between living conditions in the forecastle and the quarters of the afterguard under the poop deck. Traditionally the master's accommodation was right in the stern of the ship, where at one time long windows looked out over the vessel's wake. With the elliptical sterns of the clippers these windows disappeared and the space under their long poops was divided into a series of cabins whose size and number depended on the dimensions of the ship.

On the largest merchant vessels the master had a sleeping cabin off the roomy saloon and sometimes in addition a day cabin and an office. The mates off watch would join him for meals in the saloon, which was usually as comfortably furnished as a well appointed home ashore, with long mirrors on the bulkheads and a marble-topped sideboard railed in brass to keep dishes from sliding off in bad weather. If the master's wife travelled with him the button-backed armchairs might be decorated with antimacassars; there might even be a piano in the corner with a pot of geraniums or an aspidistra perched on top.

Mahogany or maple panelling and shiny brasswork was kept polished by the steward, who also cleaned the glass of the central skylight. This single source of light was a perpetual weakness—in stormy weather a wood and canvas cover was fitted over the panes to keep out heavy seas, leaving the room below in darkness apart from a lamp swinging in the barricaded recess.

Frequently the wind would prove too strong for the temporary cover and would whip it away over the stern, putting the fragile glass at the mercy of flying rigging-blocks or a sudden deluge of water.

If the ship was bound for Cape Horn, precautions were taken well before latitude 50° South. The Persian carpet was rolled up, a canvas cover fitted over the table and settee, and wooden slats called 'fiddles' fitted to the sideboard and the captain's desk. Weather-boards some two feet high were slotted into the base of each doorway leading on deck, and the berths equipped with lee-boards to keep their occupants from rolling out.

Below the poop the master kept a chronometer and a set of charts which were his own personal property. From the beams above his head hung an upside-down tell-tale compass as a check that the ship was on course and not straying into shoal water or along a rocky coastline.

On smaller merchant vessels the master's quarters were less splendid and his officers more cramped. The cabins of the captain and mate on a coasting schooner consisted basically of large cupboards wedged into corners of the stern with only a bunk and a small locker for a change of clothing. Between them was a tiny saloon where the crew would eat what meals they had time for at a little table surrounded by built-in bench seats. The steep ladder giving access to these quarters was a far cry from the brass-railed companionway between poop and saloon in a large merchant-man, often reserved for the exclusive use of the master. A helmsman never knew when the captain would materialise quietly on deck behind him to check the ship's course or the set of the sails, or to fix his position by the stars. Some masters hardly left the deck in bad weather, and there are many reports of tea-clippers racing back from China with the master dozing in an armchair beside the wheel, like Captain Keay of the *Ariel*.

In the isolated floating community of each ship, the master's word was law; he was judge, priest, paymaster, chief navigator and, unless the vessel carried passengers and a surgeon, he was also the only medical authority for hundreds of miles. The captain was supposed to recognise and treat diseases like yellow fever, smallpox, malaria, dysentery and sudden tropical complaints, set broken limbs, dress septic wounds and diagnose internal injuries caused by falls from the rigging. Paradoxically, amputation was considered one of the most straightforward operations, carried out with the carpenter's assistance on a suitably protected saloon table. If an open wound did go septic and then gangrenous— less likely at sea than in a bacteria-filled shore hospital—the patient might still have a better chance of survival than a man with an un-identified internal complaint. In 1867 Parliament passed an act which led to the publication of the first *Ship Captain's Medical Guide*, a Hippocratic Bible still in use, somewhat updated, today. Once diagnosis was agreed between the master and his patient the *Guide* laid down an appropriate treatment with recipes for patent medicines which could be made up from supplies on board. The steward presided over a large medicine chest containing bottles of laudanum, mercury, quinine, carbolic acid lotion, gentian violet, 'purging pills' and the basis of various numbered mixtures, but it was up to the master to follow instructions or administer other remedies of his own devising. One captain successfully rubbed frostbitten fingers with snow and packs of wet oakum—an unorthodox prescription which nevertheless seemed to be effective in the long run.

The *Guide* was designed specially for ship-board conditions, with symptoms graphically described in simple terms along with the appropriate treatment. No room was left for

The clippers *Ariel* and *Taeping* race neck-and-neck in the 1866 China Tea Race

mistakes: the passage instructing a master on the replacement of a dislocated shoulder showed him how to apply his heel to the patient's armpit, but began with a warning, 'Take off your boot . . .'

The first step in any remedy, whether for heart disease or an unidentified fever, seems to have been a dose of cream of tartar or a 'Black Purge' for 'opening the bowels'. This was even prescribed for a case of quinsy, which the master was to recognise as 'a swelling of one or both tonsils (which are small round lumps at the back of the throat)'. A bleeding nose, said the *Guide*, was nature's remedy for a headache, while a man who had inadvertently swallowed some kind of acid should be made to gulp large quantities of soap suds to dilute the poison.

In the case of ailments appearing 'from two days to a week after connection with a foul woman' the treatment seems to be designed less to cure the problem than to discourage further adventures with 'foul women'—the suffering seaman was told to soak the afflicted parts in near-boiling water, or to sit on cold metal!

Diagnosis wasn't always so accurate. In one ship's log a seaman was certified dead from 'shock', a shock sustained when one of the huge anchors fell on him! The cause of many deaths was put down as 'dropsy', which really signified that the master's powers of invention had run out and the *Guide* had failed to provide a solution. In fact, dropsy should have been quite rare on British ships due to the quantity of oatmeal carried on board.

Most large ocean-going vessels turned part of the deck into a miniature farmyard with pens of pigs and sheep and a few chicken-coops. This livestock was intended to supply the saloon with a more varied diet, but a good master saw that when a pig was slaughtered some of the meat found its way into the fore-castle. On passenger ships the animals tended to become pets, raising a general outcry when they eventually turned up on the dinner table.

Among the extra provisions which some masters tucked away in the saloon lockers was a good supply of alcohol, and there are many tales of the havoc a drunken captain could create on board. Even in his cups the master was still in absolute charge of his vessel, and the crew disobeyed him at their peril. One regular toper accidentally spilled a bucket of water over the floor of his quarters, decided the ship was sinking and kept his whole crew toiling at the pumps for the rest of the night.

For some masters in the heyday of fast passages life could be very comfortable. Bully Forbes was once paid £1,000 to take a ship to Australia and back, plus his agent's commission; this would be worth a good deal more than £10,000 today. Masters looked forward to the day when they could become ship-owners themselves and retire from the sea to a prosperous old age ashore.

But as the importance of sail declined, so did the salaries of the shipmasters, and by the end of the century many of them had grown old in sail, too old to make the transition to steam but reluctant to leave the sea. Like members of their crews who had no other home but a ship's forecastle, these men simply reversed the digits of their ages—sixty-four became forty-six, seventy-five became fifty-seven, regardless of any records which might exist. Constant exposure to the wind and sea aged every sailor so rapidly that it was always difficult to guess how old a man really was, and some seamen even helped the deception with patent hair-dyes.

One or two masters were known to have switched digits more than once. When time caught up with the new fifty-seven year-old and he 'aged' to an official figure of sixty-five, he could easily reverse the numbers again and go back to fifty-six: by this time his real age was eighty-three. Extraordinary though it may seem in these days of compulsory retirement, several cases exist of masters who suddenly dropped dead at sea, victims of sheer old age and decrepitude.

The death of its master could leave a ship in a difficult situation. The captain and first mate were usually the only men aboard capable of navigating the vessel accurately, and sometimes, since the charts were locked away

A demonstration to show how the old log-line was used. The principles of this method of determining speed at sea are described opposite

in the captain's quarters, the exact position of the ship was a secret known to him alone. Whether this was intentional or simply a result of his solitary position of command is hard to tell.

Whenever possible the position was fixed by means of a sextant, but in foggy or overcast weather a rough estimate of where the ship should be could be made by dead-reckoning. This method calculated from the speed of the ship over a given time how far it had travelled along a certain fixed course, and meant that a hand-operated log-line had to be streamed from the vessel's stern every two hours.

The log-line was a piece of wood shaped like a sector of a circle, weighted to keep it upright in the water and attached to 150 fathoms of line on a reel. The wooden board was thrown over the stern-rail and the first 90ft of line allowed to run out. When a piece of white bunting tied to the line vanished over the stern, a 28-second sand-glass was turned over while the line continued to run out in knotted 47ft lengths. When all the sand had run through the glass the line was tripped and the knots which had run out were counted, giving the ship's speed through the water in nautical miles.

In the days of the racing clippers the expression 'seventeen knots and a boy' was often used to indicate tremendous speed—in other words by the time the sand had trickled through the glass every inch of line had run from the reel, whisking the unfortunate boy on the end of it over the stern!

An experienced seaman joining a new ship would find himself on familiar territory. In spite of the apparent maze of standing and running gear each vessel was rigged on logical and universal lines; no time could be wasted fumbling for the right belaying-pin on a dark night, and a mistake might bring a royal yard crashing to the deck, carrying vital rigging with it or injuring a man below.

In addition to the shrouds and stays which supported the masts and took the strain of wind upon acres of canvas, there were numerous ropes attached to each sail for setting it to best advantage or gathering it up to its yard to be secured firmly to the spar. Clewlines, buntlines, braces, halliards, downhauls, tacks and sheets—each one had its own task to perform and its designated place on the pin-rails. 'Knowing the ropes' was no mere saying, but a practical necessity.

A large sailing ship was no place for fools, or for anyone who didn't learn from experience. A careless man on the wheel could easily allow the ship to be caught 'aback' with the wind on the front of the square sails instead of pushing from behind, putting a sudden strain on the wrong side of the masts and risking the safety of the whole ship.

The reality of going aloft was far tougher than any factual description of the work can convey. The lower yards of a large merchantman projected well over the ship's side, 50 or 60ft above the sea; the topgallant yard might be 130ft above the deck. To take in or set sail the men scrambled aloft on the ratlines between the shrouds on the weather side of the ship, the side which was uppermost when the vessel heeled over and the side which gave them the wind at their backs. Where the lower sections of each mast overlapped the shrouds converged on a wooden platform called the 'top'; to get to the next set of shrouds the men had to climb out round this platform, struggle over the edge, and go on up the rigging to the sail they were to stow.

Once level with the right yard the men worked their way out along the slippery footrope slung beneath it, clinging to the yard for support. The sail itself was bent to the jackstay, a wooden slat running along the top of the spar; to stow the vast area of flapping canvas light ropes called gaskets had to be passed round it and made fast; starting at the weather side after the sail had been gathered up in its buntlines, the men dragged the canvas up to the yard in long folds, wrapping a final skin round it to make sure the wind could find no loose corner to tear.

In bad weather this work aloft required sure footwork and an instinctive sense of balance. The wind shrieked through the rigging, tearing at tattered oilskins and wrenching the wet, billowing sail from the

men's bleeding fingers. Rain and spray made the yards slippery, wind blew the canvas rigid; in drenched jerseys and flapping trousers the seamen lay on their stomachs across the yard, clawing at the folds of the sail to bring it close enough for gaskets to be passed round it. In freezing southern latitudes the canvas became as hard as iron—nails were torn from frostbitten fingers as the men fought to subdue one huge sail.

The much-quoted saying 'one hand for the ship and one for yourself' never really worked in practice. There were few jobs that could be done one-handed; bracing themselves against squalls between yard and footrope the men struggled with the sail, grabbing the nearest hand-hold when it became necessary to save their lives.

Inevitably, many men did fall from the yards. These falls were usually fatal, although not always; men who fell into a calm sea had a better chance of survival than those who landed on a hard teak deck. Broken legs or

Furling sails on the four-masted barque *C. B. Pedersen*

(*Right*) Jessica Benton as the young Elizabeth Onedin with Michael Billington as Daniel Fogarty, a sea-captain and father of her child

ribs could be mended but more complicated injuries were almost impossible to diagnose, even if there had been some way of treating them.

Down on deck there was always the possibility of a huge sea coming aboard, knocking the watch from their feet and sending them tumbling into the scuppers. The power of these giant seas was staggering. Men could be hurled against a capstan or a pin-rail and their ribs smashed like matchwood; they could be plucked from the deck and washed away over the rail, or swept from a perilous position on the bowsprit as the ship plunged into the next wave.

Surprisingly enough very few seamen could

(*Left*) Peter Gilmore as James Onedin and
Jessica Benton as Elizabeth Frazer aboard the
brigantine *Marquès*

(*Above*) the *Macquarie*'s crew changing the
mainsail. Seamen had to know the whereabouts
of each rope in this intricate web of rigging and
running gear

swim more than a couple of strokes, but in
any case, there was no chance of a ship
fighting for its life in hurricane winds
managing to launch a boat, or putting back
to pick up a missing crew member, even if
his absence was noticed at once. With his
oilskins tied at wrists, waist and ankles—
'soul-and-body lashings'—and heavy sea-
boots on his feet, the missing man would
have drowned almost immediately. Many
seamen reluctant to learn to swim explained
that this was a kinder fate than surviving
long enough to see your ship disappear

without you towards the horizon.

If a man died on board a burial service was performed as soon as the weather permitted. A spare hatch-board was sanded smooth by the carpenter, while the sailmaker or the bosun stitched the corpse into its canvas shroud. The body was then laid on the hatch-board and carried to the ship's rail covered with a spare ensign. There the master read a burial service over the dead man and at the appropriate moment the board was tipped up, shooting the corpse into the sea where weights sewn into the canvas shroud soon took it to the bottom. As the board was tilted the bosun darted forward to snatch the ensign before it disappeared over the rail—the owners would no doubt expect it to be accounted for.

The dead men often left little in the way of personal effects—a ragged shirt, a jersey, a knife, perhaps a Bible or a pack of greasy playing-cards, depending on the seaman's inclination. An apprentice might have had

with him a book on navigation, needles and thread for repairing his uniform or a few faded photographs of his family at home.

By the end of the nineteenth century big square-rigged sailing ships were providing deck-houses for crew accommodation which were much warmer and dryer than the old forecastles in the bow, but there were still comparatively small schooners and brigantines of two or three hundred tons sailing the north Atlantic whose crews of seven or eight men lived in conditions which hadn't changed for more than a century.

It's no wonder that many seamen looked to the steamer as a better way of life at sea. When the advent of twin screws allowed steamers to dispense with sails altogether there was no longer any need to work aloft in bad weather. Great areas of open deck gradually disappeared on the passenger steamers, where the best accommodation began to be sited amidships, extending across the whole width of the vessel as on the White Star Line's opulent *Oceanic*, built in 1870. Passengers travelling in this palatial ship could spend days almost unaware of the sea but for the motion of the vessel, since there was no need for them ever to leave the shelter of cabin, saloon, smoking-room or library and brave the bracing air of the open deck.

Down in the stoke-hold the men were equally unaware of the cold sea, and the engineers tended their boilers in a clanking, thunderous heat. The invention of the compound steam engine meant halved fuel consumption; it was no longer impossible to carry enough coal for long ocean hauls away from coaling-stations, and no longer necessary to use up valuable cargo space for fuel. In less than a decade the demand for coal pushed the price up to three times its former figure, and the days of the sailing-ships were numbered.

Firemen at work in the stoke-hold of a steamer: warmer than working aloft on the yards, but no less unpleasant

8 Schooners, Steamships and Square Rig

Charlotte Rhodes is by no means James Onedin's only vessel (although with a quick change of name-plate she has been several of them—*Scotch Lass*, *Caledonia*, *Oberon*, *Cardiff*). One of the other ships often seen on the screen is the polacca brigantine *Marquès*, owned by Robin and Virginia Cecil-Wright, which 'doubled' as several more vessels of the Onedin fleet in the 1976 series.

Built in Spain in 1912, she's quite a different vessel from *Charlotte*, with two masts, sweeping Mediterranean lines, and a dark

A quick change of nameplates and the *Charlotte Rhodes* becomes the *Oberon*

Latin look about her. As a polacca brigantine she has a single pole foremast carrying three square sails, with a big fore-and-aft sail on the mainmast surmounted by a gaff topsail. Between the masts are three staysails and at her bows three headsails—a total of eleven.

Below decks twin Kelvin K4 diesels provide an alternative source of power, but apart from this comparatively modern addition and a 24-volt lighting system, *Marquès* has been restored to her original rig and fittings.

Like *Charlotte Rhodes* she's a veteran television performer; in addition to her *Onedin Line* appearances as the *Princess Alexandra* or the *Helen May*—and sometimes, with a false funnel, as the steamer *Prince Edward*—she's taken part in a *Songs of Praise* programme, *Playschool*, a BBC dramatised documentary called *The Slave Trade*, and has even played host to a pop-group called the Yetis. Her current project calls for more extensive disguise, this time as

The brigantine *Marquès,* sailing off the Cornish coast

(*Right*) two members of *Marquès'* crew work on her foreyard as she lies alongside the Old Quay, Exeter

Darwin's *Beagle* for another BBC documentary.

When the Cecil-Wrights acquired her in 1972 *Marquès* was making a regular weekly passage between Palma, Majorca and Tarragona in Spain. On the first leg of the journey she carried almonds, and on the return trip casks of wine, a leisurely and sedate employment for a sixty-year-old ship.

When he bought her, Robin Cecil-Wright planned to use the vessel as a floating base for his own documentary films, a mobile home which he could move to any part of the world where he intended to work. A short time later, however, he became firmly entrenched on a farm in Cornwall, and so far *Marquès* has been featured as much on the screen as behind the camera.

In September 1975 *Marquès* was given an opportunity to renew her old connections with the wine trade when the *Sunday Times* Direct Wine Club decided to ship 24,000 bottles of wine back from Bordeaux in the traditional way, deep in the hold of a sailing ship. For the occasion the Board of Trade granted a special dispensation from their usual restrictions on the carrying of cargo, and the old brigantine duly set off from Plymouth for the coast of France.

Because of the difficulties involved in obtaining a full Board of Trade Certificate for an old sailing vessel, Robin Cecil-Wright is sure this makes *Marquès* the current holder of the hotly disputed title of 'Last British Ship to Carry Cargo Under Sail', an argument which will rage as long as a few ships with holds still sail under the British flag. *Charlotte Rhodes* narrowly missed qualifying for this distinction in October 1976 when she left Yarmouth for Amsterdam with a cargo of marine equipment; she was then on her way to her new Dutch owner and—Board of Trade please note—was no longer a British vessel.

Hugh Johnson, a wine expert and President of the *Sunday Times* club, sailed back from Bordeaux aboard *Marquès* to sample some of the rigours of travel on an authentic cargo-carrying sailing vessel, and later described the trip in a *Sunday Times* column:

> Where am I? In a sleeping bag in a three-sided coffin smelling of tar. The charterer's quarters (charterers being expendable) are in the fore-peak of our brigantine. The bit you hit icebergs with. We sail at nine, high tide. A quick wash at the pump on deck (the last time I bothered for four days), and a dash to market for hard sausage, hard cheese, biscuits and butter. We have wine. Two thousand cases of it. The whole ship is one big cellar, which is why we are dossing with the anchor-chains and messing (the right word, that) on the engine-room hatch.

Il faut souffrir, one might say.

The passage home was complicated by heavy seas and high winds off the north coast of France which diverted the 154-ton brigantine from her intended destination of Charlestown in Cornwall to an eventual docking in Plymouth. Interestingly enough, the cost of importing 24,000 bottles of wine by this route was reckoned to be only 10 per cent above normal trucking charges.

Another ship to appear during early episodes of *The Onedin Line* was the topsail schooner, *Als*, a typical bluff-bowed Baltic trader with a square transom, which had been used as a houseboat in a previous existence. One unusual feature of her design was the letters GPO stamped on two of her masts—with great ingenuity her owners had used telegraph poles when restoring her to sail.

Like *Charlotte Rhodes*, *Als* occasionally exhibited an independence of spirit which could make life difficult for those aboard. Peter Graham-Scott recalls one day in

Dartmouth when he was alerted by a radio call from *Als* to say that her engine had broken down at sea and she was proceeding to Brixham under sail. The producer and his assistants hurried off to Brixham by road to meet the vessel when she arrived, but although they waited on the quay for some time there was no sign of the missing *Als*.

Becoming worried, the television men piled into a coastguard boat and headed out to sea to search for the errant schooner. They finally found her some 15 miles offshore, drifting helplessly in the shipping-lane at the mercy of passing tankers. Luckily her engine was soon repaired and she was able to set off back to port.

In these early days the ability to triumph over the occasional near-catastrophe seems to have been the major qualification for membership of the *Onedin Line* production team. Another heart-stopping moment was provided by the beautiful little steam-launch *Hero*, lent to the series by the giant tobacco firm of John Player and Sons.

Named after the bearded sailor of cigarette-packet fame, the 35ft launch began a new life in 1969 when she was discovered in a dilapidated state in a Somerset farmyard. Steam boat enthusiast Christopher Stirling, who found her, realised that the task of restoration would be long and expensive, and approached John Player and Sons with the idea. Fortunately they agreed to commission a refit, and the little launch was lovingly restored by Tom Trevethick in his boatyard near Nottingham.

There the rotten deck planking was removed, a new deck was built up from narrow alternating planks of oak and mahogany, and new mahogany panelled lockers were installed. At the same time the hull was strengthened and re-caulked, and a new steam-engine put in.

Now, with her sharp clipper bow of highly polished Burma teak and her gleaming brass funnel, *Hero* looks very much as she must have done when she was first launched in the 1880s.

In spite of her new-found glamour, one day in Dartmouth nearly put an end to her film career. With Peter Gilmore and Anne Stallybrass aboard, *Hero* was steaming confidently through the harbour when for some mysterious reason the little launch suddenly went out of control. With no steerage way the boat drifted helplessly upriver, straight into the path of the chain ferry which bore down on her with alarming speed. Just as the

(*Left*) the polacca brigantine *Marquès* at the Old Quay in Exeter

Transformation of the Exeter location with the ingenious placement of a few props: (*Above right*) a Victorian dock scene. (*Below right*) the Tropics

(*Overleaf*) Peter Gilmore as James Onedin and Jessica Benton as his sister Elizabeth stand outside the Onedin Ship Chandlers shop, while Howard Lang as the faithful Baines gets down to work

(*Above*) the little steam-launch *Hero*, restored to her former glory

(*Above left*) horses and carts add to the bustle on the Exeter quayside

(*Below left*) a horse and carriage waits outside the Onedin chandlery store

launch's passengers were about to leap hastily over the side and swim for it, someone aboard the chain ferry spotted *Hero*'s predicament and started to put the vessel's ponderous machinery into reverse. With inches to spare the ferry ground to a halt, towering over the high brass funnel of the launch it had so nearly trampled into the sea.

One question often asked by *Onedin Line* fans concerns the identity of the 'big white ship' which appears with *Charlotte Rhodes* in the title sequence of each episode. In fact, there are two white ships; the opening shot is of the Norwegian three-masted barque *Statsraad Lehmkuhl*, a training vessel owned

by shipping magnate Hilmar Reksten and based in Bergen. A prison ship during the war, this big vessel at one time took 600 boys a year on training cruises all over the world, and was the winner of the 1960 Tall Ships Race between Oslo and Ostend. At the moment she is laid up in Bergen harbour where the Reksten shipping line has been carrying out a process of renovation both in her 250ft hull and aloft among her massive metal spars and steel rigging. Eventually it is hoped to send her to sea as a training ship again, with the help of the Norwegian education authorities.

The other white ship of the title sequence is the Danish Government cadet ship *Danmark* which made many appearances in the first three series, under the expert control of her commander since 1937, Captain Knud L. Hansen.

Designed and built in Denmark in 1932, the *Danmark* measures 252ft from spanker-boom to jib-boom and 130ft from sea-level to the main truck. Although she has an auxiliary 486hp diesel motor to drive her through the Equatorial calms, *Danmark*'s eighty cadets are encouraged to learn to sail the three-masted full-rigger by wind alone; it has even become a point of honour to enter and leave port under sail if at all possible.

Serving on the *Danmark* confers great prestige on a would-be officer in the Danish merchant navy, and it's not difficult to fill the places available for each cruise. The boys pay for their own clothing and equipment and contribute a small token fee, the balance of the running costs being met by shipowners and the Danish Government. Although conditions aboard have improved considerably in the last forty years, the accommodation is still fairly spartan, with a small locker for each boy and a sea-chest which becomes his seat at mealtimes. In addition to normal classroom activities the boys learn about mechanical engineering, Morse signalling and radio technique, meteorology, winds and currents, ship construction and other aspects of navigation—a general grounding in skills necessary for a future officer.

Under Captain Hansen's eagle eye the *Danmark* has become a model of efficient seamanship and good discipline, a floating advertisement for her country. When she puts into port in the West Indies, South Africa, North or South America or the Canaries, it's not unusual for the pilot to refuse payment for taking the ship into harbour, or for the port authorities to waive

(*Right*) *Christian Radich*, one of Norway's three tall ships

The Danish sail-training ship *Danmark*, with her crew of cadets

harbour dues. With the captain shouting orders from the bridge by megaphone, the boys swarm up the rigging for *Danmark*'s spectacular royal salute, manning the yards with arms outstretched, a row of boys along each yard above the neatly stowed sail.

Paradoxically the graceful Norwegian full-rigged ship *Christian Radich*, which made a brief appearance in the 1976 series, is one of the youngest vessels to have been involved in the *Onedin Line*. Built just before the last war, this 575-ton steel ship was planned from the start as a sail training vessel and is now operated by the Østlandets Skoleskip organisation based in Oslo.

Christian Radich is 205ft in length with a 36ft beam and a draught of 15ft. Her main-mast is 128ft high and her sail area over 14,500 sq ft, although like *Danmark* she also has an engine capable of driving her through the water at 8 knots.

Three or four times a year the ship sets sail from Oslo, manned by six officers, eight ratings and eighty-eight cadets between the ages of fifteen and eighteen, heading for a three-month training cruise designed as an introduction to a seafaring career. As on the *Danmark* the cadets learn to work the ship, functioning as a team out on the yards or in the ship's boats and learning to stow sails, splice rope and all the numerous jobs on the deck of a sailing-ship.

For those who eventually go on to a career in merchant ships, this is probably the only real opportunity to learn about the natural forces involved in seafaring. From the storm-lashed deck of the *Christian Radich* it's a long step to the bridge of a 300,000-ton oil tanker, where the sea takes on an unfamiliar and rather distant personality.

The 'white ambassador', as she's known in Norway, has been a regular and often successful contender in the Tall Ships Race, and is a frequent visitor to ports on the eastern seaboard of North America, some-times requiring police protection from the huge crowds of sightseers pouring up the gangway.

Recently the *Christian Radich* had to make a more unscheduled stop in Britain for repairs following a bad gale off the French coast in which she lost several sails. In spite of the weather, said her commander, the cadets handled the ship like professionals.

In addition to these vessels many others have had 'sail-on' parts in the series—the Sail Training Association's *Sir Winston Churchill*, the schooner *Captain Scott*, the ketch *Tectona* owned by the Plymouth School of Maritime Studies, the 1896 fishing lugger *Moonraker* and six Portuguese rowing *chatas* owned by Exeter Maritime Museum.

For anyone other than a nationally funded institution, maintaining an old sailing vessel can be a cripplingly expensive business. Even the big sail training ships find their budgets increasing drastically year by year, and for private individuals who have lovingly worked on their own small boats to restore them to seagoing condition the rising costs of materials and labour can be a heartbreak.

Since these small craft can no longer earn a living by trading or fishing, any work provided by film and television companies means a chance to recoup some of this expense, and may even mean another sailing vessel being maintained in seagoing condition.

9 Filming the Fleet

Anyone who has ever aimed an amateur camera at a sailing dinghy knows the difficulties and frustrations of trying to take a good picture of a vessel under sail. If the sun is shining momentarily on the right side of the sails, then someone else's craft is bound to be in the way, or the boat is about to change to the opposite tack. Usually conditions become perfect when the dinghy is only a tiny speck in the distance and by the time it has worked its way up to the camera some black cloud has ruined the light.

With ordinary still photography so unpredictable, the task of trying to capture a large sailing vessel on 16mm film can be a nightmare. Those magnificent shots of plunging bows and sails glinting in the sun which thrill a television audience are in reality a tribute to the combined skills of an experienced film unit and the crew of each

Filming on board the *Charlotte Rhodes*

ship involved. Red sails in the sunset may be an artist's heaven, but they can be a film director's hell.

When the pilot programme for the *Onedin* series was being made in 1970 many of these problems were quite unknown. Producer and director knew little of how a sailing vessel was handled, and those at the wheel of *Charlotte Rhodes* had equally vague ideas about film technique.

Force-6 winds blew steadily while the unit was at sea, and gale warning cones were hoisted along the coast. Later experience showed that this was the strongest wind in which filming was possible—in a Force-7 or 8 cameras, actors and all lurched around the deck as the ship rolled, and everyone was too intent on dodging waves breaking over the bow to concentrate on remembering their lines.

Gradually the television men discovered that a sailing ship cannot come to a complete halt like a car. A ship floats on water, a moving substance subject to tides and currents which will carry it along inexorably one way

A break for lunch aboard the *Charlotte Rhodes*

or the other. Hove-to, a sailing vessel will swing broadside on to the wind; like this it will move very slowly forward and at the same time it will be pushed sideways by the wind—in other words, it's never really still. In the early days the director would position *Charlotte Rhodes* carefully in front of the camera, only to discover several minutes later when he was ready to start filming that the ship had drifted downwind and out of shot.

Similar problems arose when the director actually *wanted* the vessel out of sight. One early episode concerned an abandoned ship drifting with tattered sails across the sea. *Charlotte* was to sail up to her, round up into the wind and launch a boat to take a tow-line over to the stricken ship. Filming went well, and the unit were soon ready to take some extra shots of the abandoned vessel all alone at sea.

Charlotte was ordered away to one side, out of camera range, further and further off until at last the director was satisfied she was out of sight. In a few more minutes the extra filming was over, and the schooner was recalled for the next scene; by this time she was well downwind, and it took 45 minutes of precious filming time for her to beat back to her original position, while members of the unit tore their hair in frustration. After this a new rule was made: when a ship has to disappear from sight, it is instructed to sneak round behind the camera, not to set sail for the horizon . . .

Other problems are more immediately obvious, but no less frustrating. In the crowded waters of the English Channel there's always the chance that a modern coaster or a container ship may pop up on the horizon and hold up filming until it has passed by. As any director knows, if a minute but recognisable silhouette *does* escape his notice someone watching the programme on television months later is bound to see it and charitably draw it to the BBC's attention.

Another headache of this kind is the small-boat owner who sees something interesting going on at sea and decides to motor out for a closer look. As he gets nearer he notices that the ship's rail is lined with yelling, gesticulating people; in fact they're members of the film unit begging him to keep clear, but he probably won't realise this until the escort boat roars over to intercept him and put an end to his film debut.

One often unwanted crowd of 'extras' are the seagulls. If a flock of wheeling, screaming gulls are required for a scene in port, a few handfuls of breadcrumbs will produce them in seconds. But if a ship is supposed to be in mid-ocean hundreds of miles from the nearest land, a fat, self-satisfied gull perched on the main truck is nothing but a nuisance.

To add to a director's woes, even the most skilled captain can't whistle up a breeze every time one is needed; days scheduled to shoot storm scenes turn out to be days of cloudless skies and glassy seas, or the unit is forced to try to produce the Doldrums out of a brisk south-easterly. Life is further complicated when the filming of one 'screen' day is spread over three or four working days. If the director is really out of luck the weather can be quite different each day, so that the ship appears to be in brilliant sunshine one minute and a near-blizzard the next. Even a windchange causes problems, putting the ship on a different tack past the same cliff in two consecutive shots. It may sound like a small detail, but it can make all the difference to the authenticity of a scene.

To a certain extent the BBC can cheat the elements and bring their weather with them. Artificial fog spread across the surface of the sea will roll around very much like the real thing; the only problem is that a ship can drift out of the fog-bank before the camera has stopped rolling.

In one early episode of *The Onedin Line*, *Charlotte Rhodes* was scheduled to be caught in an official BBC blizzard, and in order to make sure everything looked realistic artificial snow was spread all over the decks, along the rail and across the hatch-covers. 'Snow' was piled on the binnacle, plastered along the yards and sprinkled on the winch in the bow. Even the shrouds supporting the masts were coated in snow.

(*Left*) getting ready to blow up a storm.

(*Above*) stuntmen falling from the rigging during the filming of *The Onedin Line* episode *Survivor*

BBC special effects experts transform a hot
August day in Devon into a Baltic iceflow

It all looked very pretty—just like a Christmas card—and in spite of the fact that it was high summer and the sun was beating down, the ship's crew and most of the cast began to shiver with an authentic chill.

In due course the filming was successfully completed, and the unit packed their bags and left for the weekend. It was only then that *Charlotte*'s crew discovered the lasting qualities of the chemical compound which had been used to manufacture the snow; far from melting it seemed to have set fast. The decks were washed down several times, the rigging hosed and the hatch-covers scrubbed, but the ship still looked as if she'd been out in a hoar frost. Repeated washing with detergents and water seemed to have no effect, and the crew were finally forced to scrape the worst patches from the rigging with knives!

One man who has been lucky with genuine weather is Douglas Camfield, who directed two episodes in the fourth *Onedin* series. For the four days he wanted windless calm off Dartmouth the elements co-operated and produced fine spring days with hardly a breeze to stir the water. This sort of weather makes filming much easier, because the ships are steady in the water, the cameras and lights stay in one place, and members of the cast can concentrate on their roles without having to worry about keeping their feet on a heaving deck.

(*Right*) with the usual crowd of sightseers, *Charlotte Rhodes* and the *I. P. Thorsøe*

Alongside Exeter Quay, the Brunel dredger, *Charlotte Rhodes* and *Marquès* line up for the camera

On the cluttered quayside, the action turns to the arrival of a horse-drawn cab, and the crews of the assembled ships can take a short break

(*Right*) like a scene from the old days: *Charlotte Rhodes*, *Marquès*, and the ketch *I. P. Thorsøe* at the Old Quay

Although as an experienced diver Douglas Camfield is used to boats and the sea he found himself with one problem he hadn't expected. For one episode which he directed, a large church bell was to be lowered over the ship's side and used as a diving-bell for vital repairs to the hull. The bell, which had already had adventures of its own before filming began, was a huge fibreglass replica some five feet high, weighted with chains and pieces of scrap iron to make it sink realistically into the water.

Unfortunately the vast bubble of air trapped inside the bell as it was lowered into the sea kept it afloat, and in spite of all the property men could do to weigh it down, the bell stubbornly refused to sink. The only answer was to drill a few discreet holes at the top of the bell to allow the air to escape as it submerged; this was done very neatly and the holes carefully disguised so that the fibre-glass bell would look absolutely genuine.

No-one bargained for the tremendous air-pressure built up inside the bell. As it disappeared into the waves the air inside rushed with a terrible hiss from the holes in the top, and big bubbles welled up underwater. With visions of a flood of letters from dissatisfied viewers Camfield spent the rest of that scene concealing his bubbling bell behind shots of the crew's intent faces . . .

Filming considerations apart, there is bound to be a certain amount of subterfuge in a television series of this kind. The budget for a programme like *The Onedin Line* is big enough without attempting to film Teneriffe *in* Teneriffe. As it happened, Teneriffe turned out to be Exeter Quay, just as the Amazon jungle appeared on the banks of the River Dart, the Cape Verde Islands were filmed in Exmouth Bay and Start Point became part of the African coast. The long-suffering cast

have dug guano on nearby Blackpool Sands and even built igloos in an old quarry in Brixham.

Weather conditions permitting, filming is done before studio work, so that film sequences can be fitted into the finished episode when it leaves the studio. Inevitably there is a time-lag between the filming of exterior scenes and the final two days which each episode spends in the television studio, and this means continuity must be monitored all the time—an actor can't appear clean-shaven aboard a ship and then suddenly bearded as he steps ashore.

Length and style of hair is another factor to be considered by the makeup department. How clean were British seamen in the late nineteenth century? How did they wear their hair? Stubble or a full beard?

All these questions have to be decided in advance, since although the makeup artists can add false whiskers or false hair, it's easier to start with the real thing, and members of the cast have to be warned in advance to let their hair grow or to give up shaving for a few days.

In the BBC studios wigs and makeup are always at hand; on location a caravan accompanies the film unit, or a building of some kind is rented to accommodate makeup and wardrobe departments. Members of the cast are dressed and made up there before they leave for each day's filming.

(*Left*) onlookers, tourists, extras, technicians, property men, makeup artists and the crew of *Charlotte Rhodes* watch a scene being filmed. And on the television screen in the end—only James Onedin and Captain Baines

Incongruously, a very modern crowd watches a scene being shot round fishing nets and a cartload of barrels

While filming was under way in Exeter the quayside was dressed by the design department to look exactly as it must have done a hundred years ago. Coils of rope and piled sails lay on the wharf among boxes, bales and wooden hand-carts. *Charlotte Rhodes* and *Marquès* lay alongside with hatch-covers off and lifting tackle rigged for loading cargo; stevedores and sailors tramped up and down the plank gangways with bolts of canvas, kegs of nails and heavy sea-chests, while on the quay nearby shipowners rolled up in stylish carriages to inspect their vessels. Wooden shop-signs were imported for the surrounding buildings and a vanload of barrels, crates, nets and creels piled up in odd corners.

Here too particular care has to be taken to keep any modern touches out of the way of the camera. Most of the buildings on Exeter Quay are old warehouses and these presented few problems, although a television aerial had to be removed from the local pub and put back again when filming was over. Funnily enough, television aerials are one of the biggest headaches for any 'period' television production, but Exeter came up with a difficulty all of its own when the BBC returned in 1976.

A new bridge to carry motorway traffic had been built over the canal connecting Exeter Basin with the sea, a product of the pile-drivers which had made life difficult during the first visit. The maximum height above water-level is about 35ft, considerably less than half the length of *Charlotte*'s mainmast, and it was obvious that to get the two vessels to the quay they would have to be dismasted.

This was no simple operation. Sails, yards and spars had to be removed first of all, then each mast supported vertically by crane while the stays and shrouds holding it in position were disconnected. The mainmast of *Charlotte Rhodes* weighs 3 tons; once the base had been dislodged from its place on the keel it was hauled slowly upwards until it was clear of the bulwarks and then moved over to the quay where a second crane was connected to the lower end and the mast lowered horizontally on to the deck. The process was repeated with the other two masts and the jib-boom which were all stowed on deck for the journey to Exeter.

In a Force-6 wind the weight of masts and spars made the schooner roll heavily as she made her way under power from Dartmouth to the Exeter Canal. There she was joined by the dismasted *Marquès*, and both vessels spent another two days replacing their masts and rigging before filming could begin. Less than two weeks later the whole process was reversed when the unit finished work in Exeter and the ships set off for home.

In April 1976, for the first time, some scenes were scheduled to be filmed after dark. No-one gets very enthusiastic about night-shooting; for actors and film unit alike it tends to be a cold business, dragged out by frequent pauses to trim the big arc lights or thaw out the cast with cups of hot coffee. In this case a mobile canteen was set up near the centre of operations to produce hot three-course meals for the forty or fifty people involved in the programme, but everyone knew there were still long, chilly hours ahead on a frosty night, with a cold wind blowing in from the river.

In coaches and cars members of the cast and the film unit converged on a little creek several miles upstream from Dartmouth. Somewhere up the steep path from the beach six or seven cows and a huge white bull were wandering inquisitively in the darkness, but the rumbling of the generator seemed to deter them from coming any closer.

Out in the river *Marquès* was anchored like a sinister shadow, her crew discussing the night's work by walkie-talkie with the director on shore; in the scenes to be filmed she was the quarantined steamer *Prince Edward*, waiting in the Mersey to take on an illicit cargo of machine parts while a troop of vigilant marines lurked nearby to pounce on

A makeup artist applies the finishing touches to James Onedin's beetling brows

Film technicians on board the *Charlotte Rhodes* during a short break in filming

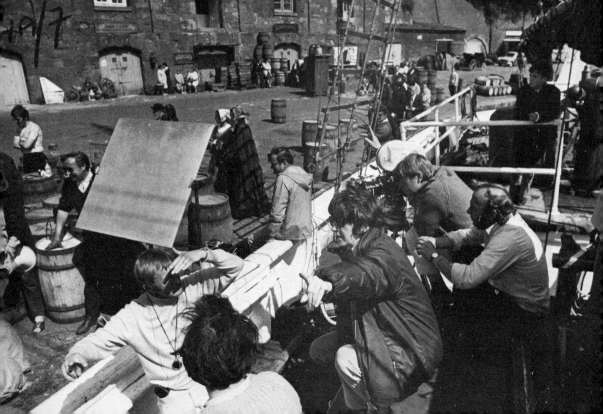

the horse-drawn carts when they reached the shore.

By midnight six bored Shire horses fidgeted in their traces on an icy beach while a handful of shivering marines hovered in the bushes, waiting for their cue to leap into action. One of the marines, it turned out later, was a girl; when she took off her cap the carefully-applied whiskers and moustache contrasted rather oddly with her pony-tail.

All over the beach members of the unit scrunched around on the shingle in wellington boots and assorted heavy-weather gear. The tide was coming in and there was only time for two more takes before the beach disappeared altogether. The property men hurriedly fed the marines' torches with more firelighters and reminded them not to lose their rifles in the undergrowth. Suddenly everything was ready; the carts began to roll heavily towards the water's edge and the marines charged out of the bushes with levelled bayonets. Something wasn't quite right, though, and the marines were sent back to charge again. This time the director was satisfied and moved on to the next scene.

At the edge of the pool of light cast by the big arcs stood a little knot of spectators who had braved the bull in the field above to watch what was going on. As time passed they vanished, frozen, into the night.

Down on the beach the Shire horses were being led out of formation and the contents of the carts piled up for collection next day. The marines had fled to the warmth of their coach, peeling off moustaches and whiskers as they ran.

(*Above right*) Brian Rawlinson as Robert Onedin and Jessica Benton as his sister Elizabeth wait to be called for the next scene. After the death of both Frazers, the pompous Robert assumed that Elizabeth would leave business matters to him, but he was speedily disillusioned

(*Below right*) Philip Bond as Albert Frazer and Jessica Benton as Elizabeth Onedin

(*Below*) near the quayside, the camera catches a confrontation between ship-owners

Out in mid-stream Peter Gilmore and Jessica Benton, as James Onedin and his sister Elizabeth, rowed reluctantly out into the gloom, urged on by members of the unit. By the time the director felt they were far enough out, they had almost vanished from sight into the darkness.

'QUIET on the beach!' yelled a voice, distorted by a megaphone.

'Quiet PLEASE! We must have ABSOLUTE quiet!'

The clumping horses were halted, everyone stiffened where they stood, and the camera rolled. Suddenly a plaintive 'Mooo-oo-oo . . .' drifted down from the field above, amplified

Michael Billington (*left*) as Daniel Fogarty and Philip Bond as Albert Frazer

Edward Chapman as Callon, James Onedin's ex-employer and bitterest rival as ship-owner

by the silent waters. Subdued titters broke out along the shore and work ground to a halt again as the director decided whether he should retake the scene.

The night wore on with frequent pauses while lights were realigned, horses placated or members of the unit ferried out to the ship anchored just offshore. With her rakish lines

and spidery rigging white in the glare of the arc lights, *Marquès* looked as if Captain Vanderdecken of the *Flying Dutchman* should materialise at any moment on her poop; the effect was so successful that even hardened technicians warming their hands at the foot of the arc lights gazed in awe across the water at the scene they had created.

When filming ended *Marquès* was to wait for the morning tide before making her way back down river, but her false funnel was needed for a different scene and had to be removed that night. It was well after two o'clock before the last of the equipment was packed up and everyone began the long trek back to Dartmouth.

(*Far left*) Ken Hutchison as Matt Harvey and Peter Gilmore as James Onedin enjoy a few minutes' rest between shots

Two views of the Old Quay, Exeter. A favourite location for filming dockside scenes until a motorway bridge restricted access to the sailing ships

Two members of *Marquès*' crew, dressed
in Victorian seamen's costume, wait for
instructions from the director

Peter Gilmore and Anne Stallybrass
stroll through a very realistic 'Victorian'
Dartmouth

The Exeter ship canal. A location chosen because
of its non-tidal waters

10 Unscripted episodes

All proper sea stories must have a skeleton, and the tale of the *Onedin* series is no exception. In this case, however, the episode wasn't so much spine-chilling as rib-tickling.

For a film unit on location every hour is expensive, and the working day begins as early as possible. When *Charlotte Rhodes* was to be involved in an *Onedin* episode she usually set off from Dartmouth at seven-thirty in the morning loaded with props for the day's filming. This meant that there were no hold-ups later on while extra items were ferried out from the shore.

One day in particular the schooner was scheduled to film scenes for the story of a drunken captain who suddenly sees the corpse of an old shipmate materialise on his yardarm. In order to give him a really good hallucination, *Charlotte* was supplied with a corpse in the form of a fully articulated skeleton on a tall metal stand. When he was wanted for filming the skeleton would be unhooked from his stand and hoisted to the foreyard, but for the time being he was set down beside the main hatch, out of harm's way.

That morning the schooner passed out through the Narrows into the Dart Estuary with her 'skeleton crew' staring blankly ahead over the bowsprit, straight and still on his metal stand. By the time *Charlotte Rhodes* was in position the sun was shining and everyone got down to work filming various preliminary scenes. When the mid-morning coffee-break arrived the neglected skeleton was still hanging stiffly on his hook, forgotten by the entire unit. Dolefully he gazed into the distance while actors, technicians and the ship's crew stood around him with cups of hot coffee in their hands.

Perhaps it was due to a fit of pique on the skeleton's part, or perhaps to the rippling wake of another vessel passing too close, but suddenly the schooner heeled steeply to one side and the metal stand with its bony passenger started to hop steadily into the scuppers.

Members of the unit watched in horror as the skeleton headed for the ship's side in a series of jolting bounds; before anyone could move, the heavy stand smacked sharply against the ship's rail, and the skull flew off to vanish with a loud *klop* into the water. Too late, everyone rushed to the rail with boat-hooks—the skull had already sunk out of sight.

There was nothing for it but to dispatch the escort boat back to Dartmouth with instructions to find a doctor who had a skeleton with a skull which he was prepared to lend.

After some time the motor vessel returned with a suitable skull which was attached to the remains of the original skeleton and the whole thing hoisted to the foreyard.

This time the property men were taking no chances, and the skeleton was firmly fixed to the foremast to prevent him shedding any more of his anatomy into the sea.

The sequel to the story occurred some months later, when the crew of a boat out fishing in the estuary discovered to their surprise that they had trawled up a human skull from the bottom. In accordance with the law the grisly find was handed over to the local coroner for official investigation, but to everyone's relief he decided that in default of any more bones it must be the same skull which had been lost from *Charlotte Rhodes* some time before. Of course, it may well have had a notice saying 'Property of the BBC'.

In fact, during the time the *Onedin* series has been running it has called for a fair amount of BBC ingenuity, both technically and on the part of individual members of the production team. One man who acted 'above and beyond the call of duty' when he was needed was Lennie Mayne, a television director who—luckily, as it turned out—describes himself as 'a bit of a water-baby'.

An experienced skin-diver of long standing, Lennie Mayne thoroughly enjoys working on programmes about the sea and ships, in spite of the extra headaches sometimes involved. At the drop of a face-mask he goes into the water himself, but on at least one occasion he found himself taking a rather unscheduled dip.

The unit had spent the day filming off Blackpool Sands, a small cove near Dartmouth hemmed in by rocky outcrops on either side. For certain intricate shots *Charlotte Rhodes* was required to anchor precisely on a certain spot just offshore where she would have to stay without moving until filming was finished. To make sure that wind and tide wouldn't alter her position a big bower anchor was dropped at her head and a kedge anchor taken out from the stern in a boat to be dropped some distance away on the end of a 300ft line. Held by these two anchors, *Charlotte* would stay at the same angle to the beach and the camera until all the complicated filming was over.

Normally the 300ft line attached to the kedge anchor would have been a stout polypropelene rope, a tough nylon fibre used on most vessels nowadays because of its resistance to rot and its ability to float on the surface of the water. However, a bright artificial fibre line leading away from the schooner's stern would look totally out of place in the late nineteenth century, so for the sake of accuracy Captain Mackreth used a heavy manilla line instead, a decision he had cause to regret later in the day.

By the time the light began to fail, filming was complete, and the cast were ferried ashore to make their way back to Dartmouth by road. Aboard the schooner members of the crew started to wind the great iron chain of the bower anchor back on its winch, a back-breaking job—it took the stout arms of four or five people to haul the dripping links aboard.

As the chain came up through the hawse-hole the schooner moved slowly forward to the spot where the anchor itself rested on the bottom; at the vessel's stern more line was paid out to the kedge anchor to compensate for this forward movement. Unfortunately the length of manilla line which had been in the water all day was thoroughly waterlogged and had sunk to the bottom. The new portion lay half-submerged under *Charlotte*'s counter.

There's an unwritten law of the sea which says that propellers and ropes have a fatal and almost magnetic attraction, and this occasion was no exception. As Captain Mac started his engine to ease the schooner gently forward and help the men on the anchor winch retrieve the heavy chain, a long loop of manilla rope wound itself round the propeller, bringing the ship to a stop.

It was soon obvious that no amount of poking and prodding with a boat-hook was going to dislodge the rope, and it began to look as if *Charlotte Rhodes* and her crew faced a night at sea. The only possible solution was to send a diver down to cut the propeller free, and eventually one of the crew rowed ashore to phone the production unit manager, Glyn Edwards, in the hope that somewhere in Dartmouth he might be able to find a diver prepared to come out at such short notice.

By good luck director Lennie Mayne was there at the time, the boot of his car full of diving equipment; delighted at the prospect of an underwater expedition he leaped into a wet-suit, grabbed a waterproof torch and set off for the stricken schooner. To the great relief of everyone aboard he slipped over the stern and into the dark water just as the sun finally disappeared over the horizon. Not only was the propeller soon disentangled from its coil of rope, but the operation was even managed without losing the anchor!

The reason for *Charlotte Rhodes'* having to anchor with such precision was a screen technique going back to the early days of Hollywood—the glass shot. On the big screen it was used in films like the Douglas Fairbanks *Robin Hood*, made in 1922, when the huge castle set designed by Wilfrid Buckland— already the biggest structure ever built for a silent picture—was made to look truly gigantic by a piece of photographic subterfuge.

In the case of the *Onedin Line* the same technique was used to create an island where no island existed. Basically, the idea is quite simple; a large sheet of glass is lined up in front of the camera, the real bits of the set and the members of the cast are filmed through it and the fake additions painted by an artist on the glass itself. If the scale is right and the edges match up, it can be very effective, and considerably cheaper than flying everyone off to a guano island.

One rescue which ended less happily for all concerned involved the schooner *Als*, one of the Onedin fleet in the early days of the series. Like *Charlotte Rhodes* and all the other vessels taking part in the filming sessions, *Als* carried smoke flares which were supposed to be dropped into the sea if anyone fell overboard. The stream of bright yellow smoke would then mark the victim's position for the waiting escort boat, which would move in to help.

One evening *Als* was returning to her moorings near the Higher Ferry in Dartmouth Harbour, a trip which took her past the Lower Ferry, Bayard's Cove and a fair portion of the old town itself. Somehow or other during her stately progress one of the emergency canisters fell from the bow and became lodged on the bobstay, the chain which runs between the bowsprit and the vessel's stem. The impact of the fall triggered off the canister's smoke mechanism, and as

Als proceeded upriver a stream of thick yellow fumes began to belch from the region of her bow.

In daylight the unnatural colour of the smoke would have been obvious to anyone watching on the Esplanade, but in the gathering dusk all that could be seen was a schooner evidently in distress, with a fire burning fiercely at her waterline. The alarm was raised, and a fire engine dashed to the rescue.

Quite oblivious to the panic she was causing, *Als* motored serenely through the harbour until she reached her moorings, where the crew set about tying her up for the night.

Meanwhile, with impressive speed and efficiency the Dartmouth Fire Brigade was following its routine for dealing with a shipboard fire. With its bell clanging the fire engine rushed off to the Lower Ferry, which was promptly cleared of the cars about to cross and turned into a fire-float. Pushed along by its attendant tug the ferry steamed at full speed past the lines of moored boats in pursuit of the burning schooner.

The firemen on board strained their eyes for a first glimpse of the distressed vessel, hoping they wouldn't arrive too late. Eventually it came in sight, moored placidly among the other boats, with not a wisp of smoke to suggest it had been a raging inferno only minutes before. History doesn't relate what was said when the improvised fire-float pulled alongside.

Considering the complications involved in marshalling a fleet of unpredictable ships in front of the cameras, it's surprising that the mishaps which have occurred have been of such a minor nature. Certainly unit manager John Fabian did land in the water when the two ships he was balanced between suddenly moved apart, and on another occasion broke his wrist after falling over a cannon; Captain Mackreth still bears the scars of a bad rope-burn when he came down from the foreyard more quickly than he intended, and one of his crew who toppled from a mooring-buoy into the river Dart had to be fished out

Director Douglas Camfield and Captain Mackreth—dressed as a Victorian seaman—discuss the next location

quickly when it turned out that he could only swim a few strokes.

But these have been the only casualties in the many episodes in the lives of the Onedins and their ships which have reached television screens in Britain and all over the world. *The Onedin Line* has sailed into homes as far apart as Saudi Arabia, Albania, Israel, Finland, Canada, Barbados, Bangladesh, Singapore, Zambia—some thirty-one countries at the last count, making the series one of the BBC's most successful exports of all time.

It's a tribute to everyone involved, both behind the camera and in front of it, the production team, designers, actors, make-up artists, scriptwriters, technicians and the crews of the various ships that a series like *The Onedin Line*, so firmly based in British maritime history, should strike a chord of recognition in countries thousands of miles away. Thanks to the painstaking research, the hours spent on attention to minute detail and the weeks spent filming in difficult conditions, the series has become a link with seafaring tradition wherever there is a receptive ear for a sailor's yarn or a heart to be stirred by the grace of a tall ship.

Glossary

Afterguard—the master and the mates

Ballast—heavy material such as stones or sand placed low down in a ship's hull to keep it stable. A ship 'in ballast' carried no cargo, but still required ballast to remain stable at sea

Barque

Belaying-pin—a wood or metal pin to which individual parts of the running rigging were made fast

Bend a sail—fasten it to its yard

Bilges—lowest part of the hull

Binnacle—a protective stand for a compass and its correcting magnets

Bitts—posts to which ropes were fastened

Bobstay—a supporting stay leading from the bowsprit to the vessel's stem

Bollards—iron posts on a quayside to which ships were moored

Boom—a spar controlling the lower edge of a fore-and-aft sail

Bowsprit—the spar running out from a ship's bow to carry the jibs

Bower anchor—one of the main anchors, fastened to the 'cathead' at the bow

Brace—a rope to control the set of a sail by adjusting the angle of its yard to the wind

Brigantine—a two-masted vessel square-rigged on the foremast, with fore-and-aft sails on the mainmast

'Bucko' mate—mate who enforced discipline with violence and bullying

Bulwarks—the sides of a ship where they rise above deck-level

Buntlines—loops of rope which gather a sail loosely up to its yard so that it can be stowed

Caulking—the sealing of seams between planks with oakum (teased-out rope) and pitch

Clewlines—ropes which haul the lower corners of a sail up to the yard for stowing

Coir—coconut-fibre used for rope-making

Counter—the stern of a ship between the waterline and its widest part

Crimp—dockland villain who preyed on shore-going sailors

'Donkey's breakfast'—rough straw palliasse

Downhauls—ropes which lower fore-and-aft sails and travelling yards in square rig

Fairleads—apertures designed to lead a rope without snagging over the ship's side

Fids—wooden spike used by a sailmaker for opening rope-strands when splicing

Fife-rail—a rack with holes to take belaying-pins

Flying-jib—outermost triangular sail at ship's head

Fore-and-aft sails—sails which have their leading edge attached to a mast or to a stay, running parallel to the line of the ship

Foremast—the mast forward of the mainmast

Foreyard—the lowest yard on the foremast

Forecastle-head—raised area of deck right in the bow

Freeboard—that part of the ship's side between the waterline and deck-level

Gaff—the spar from which a fore-and-aft sail is suspended

Gaskets—light ropes passed around a furled sail to hold it tightly to the yard

Graving dock—dry-dock where ships were repaired

Halliards—ropes for raising fore-and-aft sails or the upper yards in square rig

Harness-cask—brass-bound cask of salt beef or pork

Hawser—heavy rope of twisted strands

Heaving-line—light line terminating in a weighted 'monkey's fist' knot which was used as a messenger rope for heavier lines

Idlers—the ship's tradesmen; carpenter, sailmaker, bosun, cook

Jib-boom—an extension of the bowsprit to allow for the setting of a flying jib or other triangular sails

Kedge anchor—small extra anchor, sometimes used for moving a ship short distances

Lee shore—a coastline with on-shore winds

Lighter—small vessel used for transferring goods between an anchored ship and the shore

Marline—light, tarry, two-strand twine

Marline spike—wood or metal spike used to part strands of marline for splicing

Martingale—part of the permanent rigging under the jib-boom

Masthead—top section of mast

Mizzen-gaff—spar from which a fore-and-aft sail was suspended on the mizzen mast

Mizzen mast—mast to the rear of the mainmast

Moonsail—small square sail sometimes set above the skysail

Packet-rats—tough seamen from the hard-driven packet-ships

Palm—thick piece of leather strapped across the sail-maker's hand as a means of pushing the needle through heavy canvas and rope

Pay seams—seal seams with pitch

Pierhead-jump—a last minute leap aboard as a ship left the dock

Pin-rail—rail at ship's side pierced with holes to take belaying-pins

Poop—aftermost deck of a ship

Port-painted—custom of painting ship's side with white strip punctuated by black squares, to imitate gun-ports

Reefing sails—reducing sail-area by tying up lowest section in short ropes called 'reef points'

Royal—sail set above the topgallant

Running rigging—ropes controlling sails and yards

'Salt horse'—beef salted down in casks as provisions aboard an ocean-going ship

Scuppers—extreme edge of a ship's deck with holes through the bulwarks to drain off water

Scuttle—opening in a ship's deck with some kind of shelter over it; also, to make holes in a ship's hull in order to sink it

Sheet—rope attached to the lower corner of a sail for controlling its position

Shrouds—supporting ropes at the sides of each mast, often crossed by lighter horizontal ropes as a means of climbing the rigging

Skysail—small square sail sometimes set above the royal

'Slop chest'—Captain's store of saleable items such as tobacco and soap

Square-rigger

Standing rigging—permanent fixed rigging supporting masts and bowsprit

Stem—foremost part of the ship's bow

Stunsails—originally 'studding-sails', extra sails set on sliding booms which extended from the lower yards on either side of the ship

Tack—the ship's course to windward, determined by the set of the sails; 'tacking ship' meant pursuing a zig-zag course into the wind by passing the ship's head through the wind from time to time

Taffrail—the rail above the ship's stern, at the back of the aftermost part of the deck

Three-masted coastal schooner

Topgallant—sail set above the topsail

Topsail—sail set above the 'course' sail, the lowest sail on each mast

Transom—the flat stern of some ships above the waterline

Truck—a wooden cap fixed on top of the uppermost section of each mast to prevent rot by rainwater

'Tween deck—deck immediately below main deck

Warp—a heavy rope used for mooring a ship or for moving it by man-power

Yardarm—the outermost part of a yard, the spar from which a sail is suspended

Acknowledgements

The illustrations in this volume are reproduced by courtesy of the following:
BBC: pp 13 (bottom), 14, 17 (bottom), 29, 30, 96, 109, 112, 113, 114, 115 (top and bottom), 121, 123 (bottom), 125 (bottom), 126;
Daily Mirror, Manchester/Cyril Abraham: p 8;
David Barwick: p 7;
David Goddard, Exeter Maritime Museum: pp 9, 13 (top), 20/21, 22 (top), 23 (top and bottom), 24, 26/27, 61 (top), 91, 92, 97, 100, 102/103, 104 (top and bottom), 116, 117, 118, 119, 120, 125 (top), 127, 128;
Exeter Maritime Museum: pp 25, 99, 130, 131 (bottom);
Gillis Collection: p 56;
Hull Daily Mail: pp 34/35;
John Player & Sons Ltd: p 105;
Liverpool Central Library: p 54;
Liverpool Central Library/Stewart Bale Ltd: pp 52, 53, 69, 70;
Library of Congress Collection, Washington: pp 94/95;
Merseyside County Museums: pp 45, 51, 55, 58, 60, 77, 78 (bottom);
National Maritime Museum: 42, 53 (bottom), 87, 88, 93; (Basil Greenhill): p 67;
Nautical Photo Agency Collection: p 57;
Nicholas Toyne: pp 18 (bottom), 19, 22 (bottom), 124, 129 (top and bottom);
Østlandets Skoleskip: p 107;
Popperfoto: pp 44, 46/47 (top), 47 (bottom), 49, 78 (top), 81 (top);
P & O SN Co: p 72;
The Public Archives of Canada: p 82;
Radio Times: p 131 (top);
Robert Simper: title page, pp 12, 33, 36/37 (top), 37 (bottom), 39, 43, 98;
South Shields Public Libraries & Museums/Robert Simper: p 90;
Royal Danish Ministry for Foreign Affairs: pp 14/15 (right), 106;
Weidenfeld & Nicolson Library: pp 41, 59.

Further Reading

Readers not already familiar with the vast range of books dealing with ships and the sea might be interested to know more about the hey-day of sail than this volume can include.

Basil Greenhill's *The Merchant Schooners*, Volumes I and II—now sadly out of print— gives an excellent account of these versatile and hard-working craft, while Captain William Slade's *Out of Appledore* (Conway Maritime Press, 1972) recounts the real-life experiences of a Devon man who was both owner and master of several coasting vessels.

For a description of the most famous square-riggers, their careers and record passages, Basil Lubbock's various books reign supreme; Captain William Learmont has written two interesting accounts of voyages in the nitrate trade, and among Alan Villiers'

works is a detailed study of Cape Horn passages in the early years of this century— *War with Cape Horn* (Hodder, 1971)— compiled from his researches into the logs of the ships themselves.

The last years of commercial sail are among the best documented, and several books have been written about the famous Erikson grain fleet. Among the best are W. L. A. Derby's *The Tall Ships Pass* (David & Charles, 1970), and the vastly entertaining *Grain Race: Pictures of Life Before the Mast in a Windjammer* by Eric Newby (Allen & Unwin, 1968).

Last—but not least—avid followers of *The Onedin Line* story should read Cyril Abraham's *The Onedin Line: The Shipmaster* (Tandem, 1972).

Index